UI Design for iOS App Development

Using SwiftUI

Bear Cahill

Apress®

UI Design for iOS App Development: Using SwiftUI

Bear Cahill
Denton, TX, USA

ISBN-13 (pbk): 978-1-4842-6448-5   ISBN-13 (electronic): 978-1-4842-6449-2
https://doi.org/10.1007/978-1-4842-6449-2

Managing Director, Apress Media LLC: Welmoed Spahr
Acquisitions Editor: Aaron Black
Development Editor: James Markham
Coordinating Editor: Jessica Vakili

Distributed to the book trade worldwide by Springer Science+Business Media New York, 1 NY Plazar, New York, NY 10014. Phone 1-800-SPRINGER, fax (201) 348-4505, e-mail orders-ny@springer-sbm.com, or visit www.springeronline.com. Apress Media, LLC is a California LLC and the sole member (owner) is Springer Science + Business Media Finance Inc (SSBM Finance Inc). SSBM Finance Inc is a **Delaware** corporation.

For information on translations, please e-mail booktranslations@springernature.com; for reprint, paperback, or audio rights, please e-mail bookpermissions@springernature.com.

Apress titles may be purchased in bulk for academic, corporate, or promotional use. eBook versions and licenses are also available for most titles. For more information, reference our Print and eBook Bulk Sales web page at http://www.apress.com/bulk-sales.

Any source code or other supplementary material referenced by the author in this book is available to readers on GitHub via the book's product page, located at www.apress.com/978-1-4842-6448-5. For more detailed information, please visit http://www.apress.com/source-code.

Printed on acid-free paper

Table of Contents

About the Author

Bear Cahill has been a developer since he was 12. After getting his B.S. in Computer Science, he worked at several companies before going freelance as an iOS developer. Bear has written multiple books on software development, teaches for several corporate education companies, and develops online courses for Lynda.com/LinkedIn Learning. Ultimately, however, Bear loves to code.

About the Technical Reviewer

Felipe Laso is a Senior Systems Engineer working at Lextech Global Services. He's also an aspiring game designer/programmer. You can follow him on Twitter @iFeliLM or on his blog.

CHAPTER 1

Introducing SwiftUI

First, thank you for reading at least this much of the first chapter. It's tempting to skip it. However, I'm the type of person that reads the foreword, the preface, and so on. Someone thought it important enough to write and include it; maybe it's worth it.

When learning a new IDE, language, or user interface design tool, it can be hard to know where to start. I'll say this: if you don't know Swift, learning SwiftUI will be very tough. In fact, if you don't know about Xcode, iOS development, and the various frameworks related to it, learning SwiftUI isn't the best place to start (see Figure 1-1).

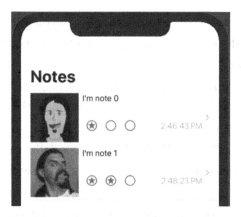

Figure 1-1. *SwiftUI Interface Example*

This isn't a book on Swift, Xcode, iOS frameworks, or UIKit. Being familiar with those is important if not required.

© Bear Cahill 2021
B. Cahill, *UI Design for iOS App Development*,
https://doi.org/10.1007/978-1-4842-6449-2_1

Exercises

I've included one or more exercises per chapter. Some are shorter and some are longer. In each case, there is also one or more End of Chapter (EOC) zip file of the code for you to review.

Many chapters build on the same code throughout the chapter. So there's only one EOC file with the full result.

The point of each exercise is practice. I want you to go through the process of employing what you're learning. I highly recommend experimenting with variations of the exercises as your curiosity prompts you.

I also strongly encourage repetition. If you repeat an exercise a handful of times to the point that you can just knock it out with familiarity, you'll be better off when you're done with this book.

Concepts

Much of SwiftUI will feel like Swift. That's good if you know Swift. You'll feel somewhat comfortable passing closures, chaining calls, handling optionals, and so on.

However, SwiftUI has a very state-driven concept to the UI. The user interface is a display of the state. If a value (the state) changes, the UI should reflect that so it needs to render again.

If the value displayed in a TextField is updated, the interface should display the new value. This is done automatically in SwiftUI with binding. We'll use property wrappers (similar to how Optional is a type with a wrapped value) to pass these values into controls like the TextField.

The TextField will be updated if the value changes. But also changes in the TextField will be stored in the same place as the item passed in. No more getting the text property and storing – SwiftUI cuts out the middle step and just changes the property!

Source of Truth

The concept of these property wrappers is tied to the idea of the "source of truth." If we have the username or email address stored in a property, that can be the source of truth. If the property changes, the UI is updated. If the user types in a new value, it's stored in that same property.

There are different ways of using this concept on value types (e.g., structs) vs. reference types (e.g., classes). We'll explore these in detail in this book.

Old Friends

We'll also look at how to use an existing UI in a SwiftUI-based app. You may have some existing code that works great, and you want to reuse it. No sense in throwing it away if it's still good.

Or you may just not have time to re-create the whole UI in one effort.

New Friends

Of course, we'll look at developing interface designs in SwiftUI. But we'll also look at how to use SwiftUI in Storyboard projects. You may want to migrate to SwiftUI starting in your current UIKit app.

However you decide or need to start using SwiftUI, I hope this book helps get you there.

Combine

If you haven't used the Combine framework yet, you will in this book. This is not a book on Combine, but parts of it are tightly integrated in things we need to do in SwiftUI.

There are Combine aspects sprinkled throughout this book. There's also a chapter specifically intended to go a little deeper into Combine. That framework probably deserves its own book, but we'll dig a bit deeper at times to understand what we're doing and using.

It's All Good

As mentioned, the code is the UI. It doesn't get stored as XML or something, for the UI to get generated from.

But also, the Canvas is the simulator. When you go into Live mode, it's effectively the same as the simulator. It's not perfect, but you can be sure it's close. Also, it's much more than just viewing a rendering of how it's designed without the underlying code (like the Storyboard Preview).

You can even design your preview to display for various color schemes, devices, and so on (see Figure 1-2).

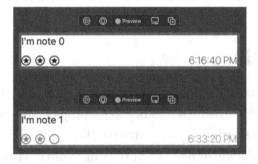

Figure 1-2. *Multiple Previews of One Element*

The key thing for me here is that we need to rethink how we think of the user interface. Instead of creating items with attributes, we call modifiers on those items. They in turn return items, and we repeat as we chain the calls together.

Our UI is tied to our state, and they stay in sync. Changes to the state update the UI. Changes in the UI update the state.

If you're not careful, that may mean everything is tightly coupled. But we're going to break things down and use a lot of functionality built into SwiftUI. In the end, we'll see that many aspects of the interface work the same. So in the past, what took several building blocks can now be done with one or two.

Platforms

We'll be focusing on iOS development with SwiftUI. However, in many cases, the code is the same for the Apple Watch, macOS, iPadOS, Apple TV, and who knows what's coming.

We'll look at a couple examples of the UI from iOS copied into a watch project. The changes will be minimal to get it to work. SwiftUI is a bit more abstracted. Tell it to render a Picker, and it will figure out what that means given the platform.

Let's Get to Codin'

Hazzah!

CHAPTER 2

Take It Easy

In this chapter, we'll ease into SwiftUI by seeing it in action. If it feels slow, good! The beginning is the only time to lay a foundation and that needs to be solid. Rock solid. Like math, a spoken language, or many other skills, if we don't get this down now, we'll be lost later.

Code + UI

If you've done UI development in Xcode in the past, you know that combining the UI design and code is possible. However, they aren't hot swappable. You don't change a background color to red in the code and then open Interface Builder and see that change. At least, now without some special coding.

With SwiftUI, you can think of the code and the UI as one thing. Effectively, it is. In the past, the UI was translated into XML. That wasn't very readable nor easy to edit correctly. Now the UI is generated from the SwiftUI code. As you make changes to the code, the preview is updated to show the changes.

Moreover, if you modify the UI in the preview canvas, it updates the code. Let's look at an example starting with a new project.

© Bear Cahill 2021
B. Cahill, *UI Design for iOS App Development*,
https://doi.org/10.1007/978-1-4842-6449-2_2

YOUR FIRST SWIFTUI APP

We're going to start by creating a project from a template, analyzing what's created, and changing the UI for our purposes.

1. Open Xcode and start a new project (Figure 2-1).

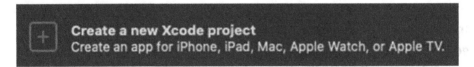

Create a new Xcode project
Create an app for iPhone, iPad, Mac, Apple Watch, or Apple TV.

Figure 2-1. *Create New Project Option in Xcode*

If Xcode is already running, select File ➤ New… ➤ Project (⇧⌘N).

2. Select the iOS App template and click Next (Figure 2-2).

Figure 2-2. *iOS App Template*

3. Set your product name and other details including the Language (Swift), User Interface (SwiftUI), and Life Cycle (SwiftUI App) (Figure 2-3).

Figure 2-3. *Project Options*

4. When your project is created, preview updating may be paused.
    If so, click the Resume button (Figure 2-4).

Figure 2-4. *Resume Automatic Preview*

Once the preview updates, ytou'll see your first SwiftUI. Congrats. No one is
more proud of you than me.

Hello SwiftUI

Of course, this is the typical "Hello World" example. Let's look just briefly
at what we have line by line.

We're importing SwiftUI on line 9. That's new. That's where the various
SwiftUI items are defined obviously.

On line 11 is the first line of code for our new app. We have a struct called ContentView which implements a protocol named View. We can see the definition of view with ^ ⌘ + click "View."

So anything implementing View needs to have a property called "body." That property must have a getter that returns the type specified by the associatedtype of the Body: something that implements View.

Back in our code, we see that ContentView implements View. The return type is "some View," and the body of that computed body property is a Text.

Note   We'll get into the "some View" and opaque types later. For now, just know that whatever is returned from our body computed property must implement View.

You've probably already guessed that Text is like a label. We create it with a String, and there it is on the UI.

Modifiers

As with other methods of UI development, SwiftUI elements can be modified. Text has modifiers like font, color, alignment, and so on.

We can add a modifier to our Text element to make the font red like this (Figure 2-5):

```
Text("Hello, World!")
        .foregroundColor(.red)
```

Hello, World!

Figure 2-5. *Text with Red Foreground*

And you'll notice the UI updates in the preview.

Similarly, we can bold our text by chaining another modifier. We may want to split these onto multiple lines for the sake of cleanliness (Figure 2-6).

```
Text("Hello, World!")
    .foregroundColor(.red)
    .bold()
```

Hello, World!

Figure 2-6. *Text with Bold, Red Foreground*

As you can imagine, there are many visual variations you can have on a given UI item. That translates to a lot of modifiers with many parameters. It's a lot to learn and remember.

SwiftUI Inspector

Fortunately, you don't have to remember all of the modifiers. Xcode is here to help!

If you ⌘ + **click** the Text item, you'll see a pop-up menu. From that, select "Show SwiftUI Inspector..." (Figure 2-7).

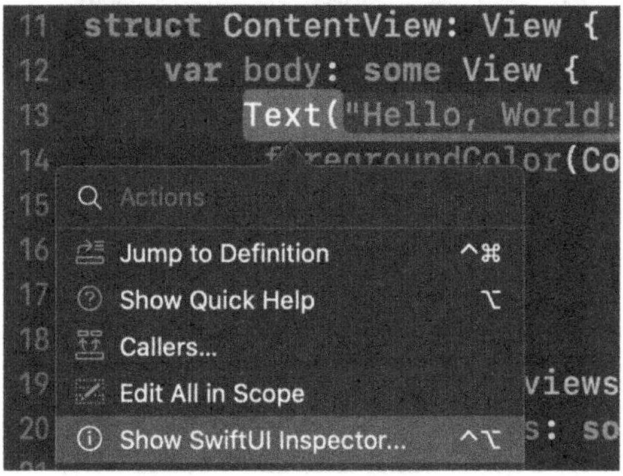

Figure 2-7. *SwiftUI Inspector Menu Item*

Note   You can alternatively ^ ⌥ + **click** the Text and go right to the SwiftUI Inspector.

Once the SwiftUI Inspector is displayed, we see that there are a variety of attributes we can set with modifiers.

Not only that, but we can add modifiers with the drop-down at the bottom (Figure 2-8).

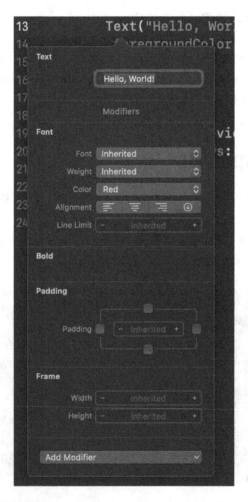

Figure 2-8. *SwiftUI Inspector*

As you make selections on these controls for the modifiers, your code is updated to reflect the choices you make.

Note the empty section titled Bold. That's there because we manually put in that modifier, but there are no settings for it.

The better way to bold the text would be through modifiers in the Font section of the inspector.

Exercise time!

MODIFY WITH MODIFIERS

In this exercise, I want you to use modifiers in the SwiftUI Inspector to get your "Hello World" text to match the following example. Give it a shot on your own before reviewing the steps. Also, remove the .bold() line of code to have a better starting place.

```
Text("Hello, World!")
    .foregroundColor(Color.red)
```

Here's what I want your text to look like by only using the SwiftUI Inspector (Figure 2-9).

Figure 2-9. *Updated UI Preview*

You can easily see several things have changed:

1. Text ("Hello, SwiftUI!")

2. Font color

3. Font size

4. Font weight

5. Spacing of the words

6. Size of the Text

7. Background color

8. Corner radius

Feel free to play around with the various modifiers and settings of their values. Practice with these types of things will make you more comfortable and natural in making these changes.

Ideally, you'll get to where you don't have to stop, think, wonder, and search for the right settings.

Here's the resulting settings in the SwiftUI Inspector I used to get the Text item the way I wanted it:

I made three changes in the Font area: the font itself, the weight, and the color.

I changed the padding to 30 (you can edit the number directly by clicking it).

I also changed the frame's width and height manually to 200 and 400, respectively.

I used the Add Modifier drop-down list to add two other modifiers: Background and Corner Radius. Once added, I was able to set their values.

Here's what the code looks like after these changes:

```
Text("Hello, SwiftUI!")
    .font(.largeTitle)
    .fontWeight(.bold)
    .foregroundColor(Color.purple)
    .padding(30.0)
    .frame(width: 200.0, height: 400.0)
    .background(Color.orange)
    .cornerRadius(40.0)
```

Again, please get comfortable using these controls and associating the changes with the code and UI. Next, we'll look at some other ways to do these tasks.

Attributes Inspector

You can ^ ⌥ + **click** the UI item like you can on the Text in the code. However, the SwiftUI Inspector may not look the same.

Notice, in this case, there's only a couple of options available in the pop-up (Figure 2-10).

To see all of the same modifiers you saw before, the Attributes Inspector is a reliable option.

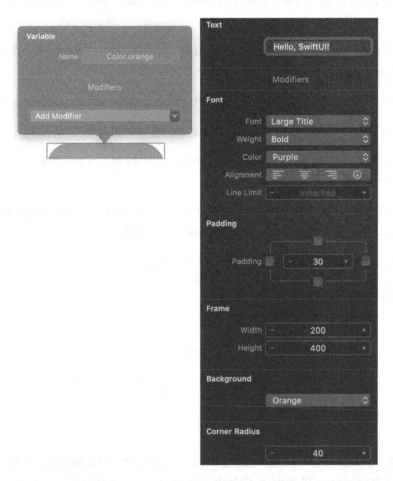

Figure 2-10. *Pop-up Menu in the Canvas*

ATTRIBUTES INSPECTOR

In this exercise, we'll see that the same modifiers can be accessed via the visual UI design in the Canvas. However, there's no need to shift your mind from "working in code" to "working in the UI." They are the same. The code is the UI.

1. Open the Inspector Pane (on the right) with this button on the top right of the Xcode window (Figure 2-11).

Figure 2-11. Inspector Pane Button

2. Select the Attributes Inspector at the top of the Inspector Pane (Figure 2-12).

Figure 2-12. Attributes Inspector Tab

3. Click the "Hello, SwiftUI!" Text item in the UI or in the code to have the attributes show up in the Attributes Inspector (Figure 2-13).

Figure 2-13. *Attributes Inspector*

If not all of the modifiers show up, click the item in the code.

Notice that the values are the same as before. Also, the Add Modifier drop-down list is available.

From here, you can make the same choice and changes.

4. Change the background color, text, and other settings and verify the changes in the UI and code.

You probably see that there are various ways to do the same things. You can edit code, make changes in the SwiftUI Inspector and in the Attributes Inspector.

And hopefully you're thinking of the code and the UI as one thing: ideally that the code *is* the UI.

Stacks of Stacks

A screen in an app with only one element isn't much of a user interface. Nor is it common. But there's only one element returned from the computed body property. What are we to do?

Most of the time, the one item we return will contain many other items. So it's a container of other items. And as we'll see, it's often a container of containers of items and so on.

Two common containers we'll see are horizontal stacks (HStack) and vertical stacks (VStack).

Horizontal stacks stack horizontally. You can probably guess that vertical stacks stack vertically. If you're familiar with the stack view from Interface Builder, you're probably already where I'm going.

One easy way to embed an item into a stack is via the pop-up menu from ⌘ + **click** (see Figure 2-14).

Figure 2-14. *Context Pop-up Menu with Embed Options*

This simply wraps an item in the code with applicable HStack or VStack code. This is what it looks like to wrap it in a VStack:

```
var body: some View {
    VStack {
        Text("Hello, Swift")
            .font(.largeTitle)
            .fontWeight(.bold)
            .foregroundColor(Color.blue)
            .padding(30.0)
            .frame(width: 200.0, height: 400.0)
            .background(Color.green)
            .cornerRadius(40.0)
    }
}
```

You shouldn't notice a change in the UI we had before because there's only one item in the stack. The way we had the UI before with one item would put it in the center. The same is true for the new stack.

However, if we add more items (e.g., another Text item below the current one), it will stack them vertically.

If I add another Text item below the current one, it would look something like Figure 2-15.

Here's the Point

I hope you're starting to see how this part is working. We have the code and UI – boom – as one! The UI is built off of the code, not like in the past where you instantiate a button, set its attributes, and add it to the screen (Figure 2-15).

Figure 2-15. *UI with Additional Text at the Bottom*

Now we have code built into the framework that is expecting you to do the UI via code. Because of things like the View protocol, a body computed property returns "some View," and that is displayed.

So we have to implement that to return something that adopts the View protocol. Text and other items do, so we can create those to return.

Also, single-expression closures automatically return the result of that expression. So we can just get to codin'!

Whether we create a Text item or a VStack or HStack with items in them, it will get returned.

For the items we create, we can add modifiers to change the colors, spacing, font, padding, and so on. These can be added in the code or via the Inspectors.

The SwiftUI Inspector can be displayed via the menu with ⌘ + **click** or opened directly with ^ ⌥ + **click**.

The Attributes Inspector is displayed via the right pane (Inspectors) with the Attributes Inspector tab button selected. Each item selected in the UI or code will show the attributes related to that item. In some cases, selecting the item in the code is best.

USER INTERFACE EXERCISE

I want you to use your existing project (or feel free to create a new one) and make the UI look like the image (Figure 2-16).

Figure 2-16. *UI for the Exercise*

In the following, I'll give you some hints and after that the solution. But first, try to recreate this look by adding items and modifiers to see if you can get the look right.

There are also some hints in the text itself.

Here are the hints:

- All three items are Text items. Nothing new there.

- The second item only has one modifier: .border

- The third item has two modifiers mentioned in the text: .padding and .opacity

- The three items are contained within a VStack.

I hope you got some good exercise adding items and modifiers. I want to encourage you to always experiment. Try adding modifiers like Blur or Shadow and see how it works.

Here's the solution code:

```
VStack {
    Text("Notes")

        .fontWeight(.bold)

        .foregroundColor(Color.white)

        .padding(30.0)

        .frame(width: 300.0, height: 50.0)

        .background(Color.blue)

        .cornerRadius(15.0) Text("This has a red border.")
        .border(Color.red, width: 1)

    Text("This has a black background but opacity of 0.5. It has
    multiple lines but doesn't go off the screen and is left
    justified. It also has some padding to keep from the edges
    and the item above.")

        .foregroundColor(Color.white)
```

```
    .background(Color.black)

    .multilineTextAlignment(.leading)

    .opacity(0.5)

    .padding(45)

}
```

Chapter Summary

In this chapter, we considered the mind shift related to SwiftUI coming from other concepts. SwiftUI code *is* the UI just as much as a nib/xib/storyboard XML was the UI in the past.

We looked at the View protocol and the defined computed property of the body of that type.

We inspected a template definition of a single-view app. The ContentView struct implements the View protocol with a single-expression closure of a Text element.

Using the SwiftUI Inspector and Attributes Inspector, we saw how to add and change values on modifiers. And using the pop-up menu, we saw how to embed an item in a VStack or HStack.

In the next chapter, we'll move beyond just the basic Text element and use a wider selection of the various UI elements provided to us for UI development.

CHAPTER 3

SwiftUI Building Blocks

In this chapter, we'll look at the variety of building blocks provided by SwiftUI. SwiftUI, like UIKit, provides various elements we can use to build out our UI. We've already seen the Text UI element. That's just the start.

Old Friends and New

If you've worked with Xcode development before, you're probably familiar with many of the standard UI elements. Switch, Segmented Control, Picker View, and others have been good friends for a long time.

Don't worry – you'll still be seeing them. However, you'll create them differently. Of course, yes, it will be in code. But it will also take a more declarative approach. Declarative in the sense that you'll tell SwiftUI what to do, but not necessarily how to do it.

Let's take a look at Button.

Button

Nearly every UI includes a button somewhere. The user taps on it and code is executed. Simple. It implies the functionality to a degree. Buttons primarily need two things: what code to call when tapped and what to display on the button (text, image, or both).

So let's do that now!

© Bear Cahill 2021
B. Cahill, *UI Design for iOS App Development*,
https://doi.org/10.1007/978-1-4842-6449-2_3

```
┌─────────────────────────────────────────────────────┐
│                CREATE A BUTTON IN THE UI              │
└─────────────────────────────────────────────────────┘
```

In this exercise, we'll add a button to the UI using the keyword Button. We'll call an initializer to pass in what code to call and what to display on the button. In this case, we'll use text.

1. Open a project (existing or new) and click the ContentView. swift file for editing. I'm using existing code, and my body property currently looks like Figure 3-1.

```
13        VStack {
14            Text("Hello, Swift")
15                .font(.largeTitle)
16                .fontWeight(.bold)
17                .foregroundColor(Color.blue)
18                .padding(30.0)
19                .frame(width: 200.0, height: 400.0)
20                .background(Color.green)
21                .cornerRadius(40.0)
22            Text("another item")
23        }
24    }
```

Figure 3-1. Computed Property Body Contents

I have a VStack vertically wrapping two Text items.

I want to add a button between the two Text items with code to call right inline where I define it. You can also provide a method name to call instead of creating a closure.

2. Type "Button(ac" (This awkward looking text specifies which Button initializer we want for code completion.) below line 21 (Figure 3-2). Notice the two parameters for the action (code to call) and label (what to display – implements protocol View which we discussed in the previous chapter). Press Return to auto-complete the code.

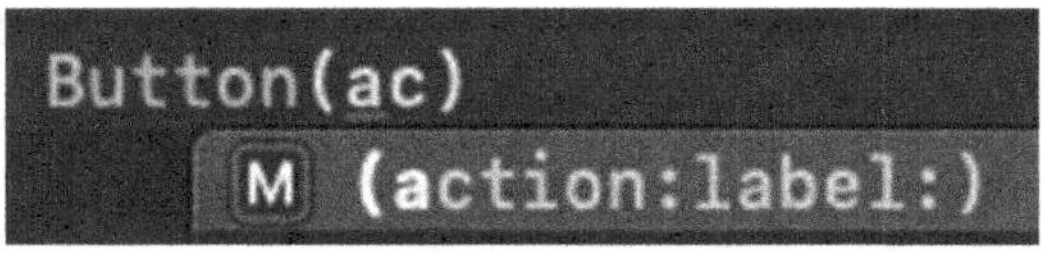

Figure 3-2. *Button Auto-complete Code*

For the code, we'll define it inline, so tab until the code placeholder ("()
-> Void") is highlighted (blue in my case) and press return to stub out the
closure.

We don't want to run any real functionality yet so we'll just put in some
dummy code.

3.   Type "`print("tapped!")`" in the body of the closure
     (replacing the "`code`" placeholder).

The second parameter, Label, is a generic in Button required to implement the
View protocol. We saw this in the last chapter with the Text item. Similarly, its
modifiers return that type so we can chain them together.

We might want to display an image on the button or a variety of other items.
But text is common so we'll use a Text element.

4.   Replace the second parameter placeholder with a single
     expression closure returning a Text item. This implements the
     View protocol so it matches the return type.

The code now between the two previous Text items should look like this:

```
Button(action: {
    print ("tapped!")
}, label: { Text("Tap Me") })
```

The preview should also now include a button between the two preexisting
Text items. Notice that the VStack is just placing the items in top-down order.

We can expect that if we run this code (⌘R) in the simulator or on a device, we can tap this new button (Figure 3-3). Also, we should see the output ("tapped!") printed to the debug output console.

Figure 3-3. *UI as Designed*

5. Give it a shot! Run it and tap the button for the output.

What did we do in this exercise?

In an existing (or new) project, we added a button. To create the button, we used the Button struct initializer with two parameters.

The first parameter is the closure (inline or method name) that takes no parameters and returns no value. The second parameter implements View – this is the visual part(s) of the button. We used Text which, as we saw in the previous chapter, satisfies that requirement.

The preview shows our new button, and executing the code allows us to tap the button and see the output. Easy!

Bonus: I encourage you to play around with the various modifiers on the button. You can apply modifiers to the button itself or the second parameter UI item (the Text item in our case). See what the rotation effect (.rotationEffect) does – you can use .degrees to create the angle to pass in.

Button Parameters

We saw that a Button takes two parameters: action and label. Action is the closure for the code to execute when the button is tapped. Label is a closure that returns the UI (something that implements the View protocol) to display on the Button (typically a Text or Image).

Let's look at Image next.

Image

Another common user interface item is something that will display an image. In UIKit, it's UIImageView. With SwiftUI, it's named Image and it implements the View protocol. Just like Text or Button items, an Image can be returned as a View return type.

SF Symbols

To display an image, we start by typing Image. We have a few options after that including providing the name (the image file's name from an Assets catalog) and systemName (see more information about SF Symbols here: `https://developer.apple.com/design/human-interface-guidelines/sf-symbols/overview/`).

Let's create an Image item using the system name "camera."

31

ADD AN IMAGE

In this exercise, we'll add an image to our UI with the Image struct. This, like the past items we've seen, implements the View protocol.

1. Open a project (existing or new) and click the ContentView. swift file for editing. I'm using the existing code from the last exercise.

2. Add an Image item at the bottom of the body property using the initializer that takes a system image name. Pass in "camera" for the parameter value. The code should look like this:

```
Image(systemName: "camera")
```

3. Resume the preview if necessary and verify the image is displayed (Figure 3-4).

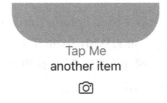

Tap Me
another item

Figure 3-4. *Camera Image in the UI*

Your UI should now have an image displayed. If you used the existing code, your UI should have the image below the other visual elements.

Feel free to add more Image items and use another system image names. Add an image to your Assets.xcassets catalog and display it with code like this:

```
Image("brainwashIcon")
```

You may also want to set its size. Use the Resizable modifier and then the Frame modifier to set the size:

```
Image("brainwashIcon")
    .resizable()
    .frame(width: 100, height: 100,
          alignment: .center)
```

Also, experiment with various modifiers. Check out the Color Invert modifier (`.colorInvert()`). Notice there are initializers for the Image that take other values including Text. See what those do!

Image Creation

The core ability to display an image is based on specifying which image to display. We created an image using a system name (SF Symbols). You can also create an image with a name of an image from an assets catalog. There are other options and modifiers you can use to customize the appearance.

Toggle

Toggle a great place to point out the declarative nature of SwiftUI. When creating a switch, we don't use "Switch" or "UISwitch." We cut to the declarative version of "what to do" over how to do it. So we use Toggle.

Using the term toggle tells the system what we're trying to do: provide an on/off-type control to the user. Here, you see there's an initializer that takes two parameters (Figure 3-5).

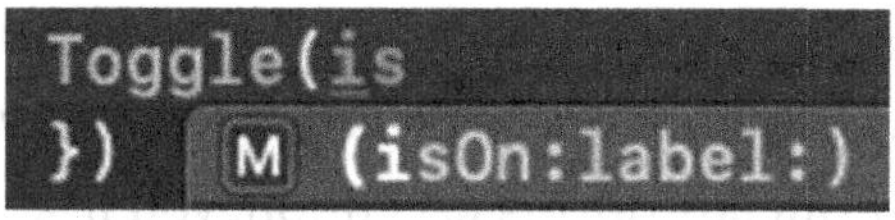

Figure 3-5. *Toggle Auto-complete*

The declaration shows more details of the initializer.

```
public init(isOn: Binding<Bool>,
      @ViewBuilder label: () -> Label)
```

The first parameter is the initial state of the toggle: on or off. But notice it's not just a Bool. The parameter type is Binding specifying the generic being used is a Bool.

The second parameter, like with the Button, is a generic named Label. The Toggle code defines that this generic conforms to the View protocol.

Binding

We'll get into how this works in later chapters. For now, understand that it's binding the parameter passed in to the UI. So if the value of the property (e.g., isReady) changes, the Toggle needs to update too.

Further, if the Toggle needs to update, the UI needs to update so it's re-created and redisplayed.

So the Toggle and the property are bound together. When one changes, the other changes.

We declare the property like this:

```
@State private var isReady : Bool = false
```

@State Property Wrapper

In order to bind our property, isReady, to UI elements, we need to use the @State property wrapper. This does a few things for us.

It creates a wrapper for the property. So, while isReady is set to false and even declared as a Bool, accessing it is done via the wrapper. In fact, if you drill down into isReady during execution, you'll see something like Figure 3-6.

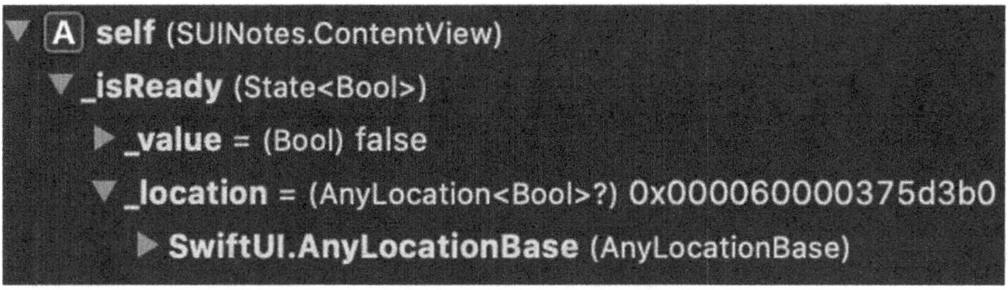

```
▼ Ⓐ self (SUINotes.ContentView)
  ▼ _isReady (State<Bool>)
    ▶ _value = (Bool) false
    ▼ _location = (AnyLocation<Bool>?) 0x000060000375d3b0
      ▶ SwiftUI.AnyLocationBase (AnyLocationBase)
```

Figure 3-6. *Property Wrapper in the Debugger*

Notice the State<Bool> as the type. The value is stored below that. Also, the location is stated as SwiftUI. That's because the UI is storing and managing the value.

@State is meant for creating a "source of truth" for a value that is specific to one view. That's why we also see it marked as private – it's only for this view. That's recommended.

To create the binding in the UI, like for our Toggle, you add the prefix $ to the property (e.g., $isReady). In other ways, like checking the value or setting it programmatically, you do it as usual (e.g., somewhat like an Optional: isReady = true).

The key thing to understand here is that instead of the action on a Toggle setting a value, we're binding the value. So we've handed to the Toggle our value to update. Moreover, if the value changes otherwise, the Toggle is updated visually.

Toggle Label

The second parameter is a label. This is basically the same thing as we saw with the Button. The second parameter is what to show. In this case, it displays it next to the Toggle as opposed to on it like the Button did.

If you look at the declaration of that Label parameter, you'll see this comment:

```
A view that describes the effect of toggling `isOn`.
```

This is great! It's letting us benefit from the existing element definitions and appearance. If the standard Toggle changes later or is used on another device, it can adapt based on that system. If you design this for an iPhone but build it for an Apple Watch later, the UI will adapt.

We just need to declare what we want (i.e., Toggle) and bind it to the property it represents (i.e., isReady) and whatever UI we want displayed describing the effect of toggling (e.g., Text).

What we're really trying to provide is something that goes along with the toggle to describe what it does. So... let's...

TOGGLE EXERCISE

In this exercise, we'll add a Toggle to our UI. It's going to be bound to a property so we'll add that to our ContentView as isReady which will be a Bool.

1. Open a project (existing or new) and click the ContentView. swift file for editing.

2. Add a property just above the "`var body...`" property line:

   ```
   @State private var isReady = false
   ```

This creates a property wrapper for isReady's Bool value with an initial value of false.

3. Edit the body computed property and add a Toggle at the bottom of the returned value. It has two parameters:

   1. isOn – Passes in the binding of isReady with

      ```
      $isReady
      ```

2. label – Passes in a Text item to display for the Toggle. Your Toggle code may look something like this:

```
Toggle(isOn: $isReady,
        label: {
            Text("Ready: " + (isReady ? "Yes" : "No"))
})
```

In this case, the Text will also indicate the value of the setting. That would probably be redundant in an actual app, but for our purposes, it's the verification of the value.

4. Run your app and verify that initially the Toggle is off because isReady is false (Figure 3-7).

Figure 3-7. *Toggle Set to Off/False*

5. Turn the Toggle on and verify the Text element is updated to include "Yes" (if you defined a similar Text element to the above) (Figure 3-8).

Figure 3-8. *Toggle Set to On/True*

6. Add a Button (or modify an existing Button) and toggle the isReady value when the button is tapped.

7. Run the app and verify that when the button is tapped, the UI updates with the toggled value.

Hopefully, you were able to complete this exercise easily and saw the same results and more!

Code as of Now

Here's my current code for my body property through all of these exercises including an Image for a png file in my assets catalog:

```
var body: some View {
    VStack {
        Text("Hello, Swift")
            .font(.largeTitle)
            .fontWeight(.bold)
            .foregroundColor(Color.blue)
            .padding(30.0)
            .frame(width: 200.0, height: 400.0)
            .background(Color.green)
            .cornerRadius(40.0)

        Button(action: {
            print ("tapped!")
            self.isReady.toggle()
        }, label: { Text("Tap Me") })

        Text("another item")

        Image(systemName: "camera")
        Image("brainwashIcon")
            .resizable()
            .frame(width: 100, height: 100, alignment: .center)
            .colorInvert()

        Toggle(isOn: $isReady,
                label: {
                Text("Ready: " +
                        (isReady ? "Yes" : "No"))
        })
```

```
    .padding([.leading, .trailing], 100.0)
  }
}
```

And Figure 3-9 shows what it looks like in the preview.

Figure 3-9. *Current SwiftUI Code in a Canvas*

A few things worth noting:

- The Button action prints "tapped!" and toggles the isReady value.

- The second Image item has three modifiers on it. The resizable modifier's output has .frame called on it.

- I also called .colorInvert on the same Image. This can be called on the Image, but its return type doesn't respond to .resizable(). In some cases, the order matters.

- The Toggle uses binding for the isOn value, but otherwise isReady is treated like a normal property.

- I used .padding on the Toggle to get it away from the sides.

TextField

One other control that is very common also is the TextField. It allows users to type input in whether it's a name, email, phone number, password, or other text-based values.

There are other UI controls used for user input, but the ones we've covered plus the TextField are probably the most widely used.

If we bring up the View Library (+ button on the top right (see Figure 3-10) or ⌘⇧L), we can add a TextField.

Figure 3-10. *Object Library Button*

Next, filter by "text" and we'll see listed the Text item and TextField item. From here, we can drag the TextField into our UI via the Preview pane (Figure 3-11).

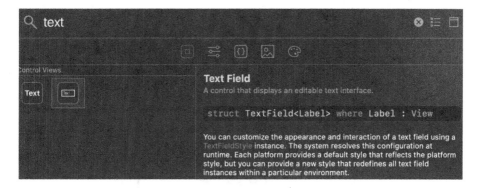

Figure 3-11. *TextField in the Object Library*

The code is updated (based on where in the order of UI elements it's dropped) to include

```
TextField("Placeholder", text:Value)
```

This Value is a placeholder. If you look at the .swift file in another editor, you'll see it contains some markup language for Xcode. This Value placeholder resolves to an empty string (""). In this case, you can actually compile and run this code with any changes:

```
TextField(/*@START_MENU_TOKEN@*/"Placeholder"/
*@END_MENU_TOKEN@*/, text: /*@START_MENU_TOKEN@*//
*@PLACEHOLDER=Value@*/.constant("")/
*@END_MENU_TOKEN@*/)
```

I put the TextField at the top of my VStack so that the keyboard would be far away from covering it up (See Figure 3-12).

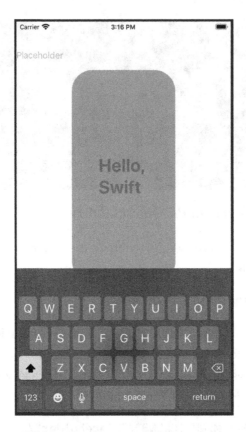

Figure 3-12. *TextField in the User Interface*

I'd like to do a few things to make this TextField more like we'd expect. First, I want to replace the placeholder text. I'll change the Placeholder to something like Name, Email, or similar. Also, I want to add some padding to get it a little bit away from the sides. Finally, I want to bind a property value to the text.

Binding in this case is very similar to the Toggle. We'll create a String property with a @State property wrapper. Then we'll use the $ prefix to bind it to the text parameter for the TextField.

Let's try that as an exercise. I'll list out what to do, and you see if you can do it without the steps...

ADD A TEXTFIELD

Here are the goals of this exercise in a list. First, try to accomplish these things without looking at the steps. Whether you get it done or not, check out the following details once you're ready.

Goals:

1. Open your ongoing project (or create a new one).

2. Add a property to your ContentView struct. It should be

    1. An @State property wrapper

    2. Declared as private

    3. A variable

    4. A string

    5. Named username

    6. Defaulted to empty string ("")

3. Add a TextField by dragging in from the View Library.

4. Set the placeholder for the TextField to be "Username".

5. Set the text parameter for the TextField initializer to a binding of the username property.

6. Add padding to the TextField with a value of 30.

7. Bonus: Use the .disabled(Bool) modifier on another UI element. Pass in as the Bool value that the length of self.username be 0 (i.e., if there's no user input, the other control should be disabled).

Hopefully, you were able to complete this exercise without much trouble. We're putting together more and more items and concepts. And we'll continue to build on these over time.

Depending on your starting point, your UI may look something like Figure 3-13.

Figure 3-13. *Starting UI for the Exercise*

It doesn't look too much different really than just a pointless TextField. But we know that behind the scene, it's bound to the username property. So if that property changes, our TextField will need updating, and the whole UI will be re-rendered.

Also notice that the "Tap Me" button is disabled. This is because the username length is 0. Once the user types in the TextField (or the username value changes in some other way to not be blank), the button will enable.

Here's the steps:

1. Add the property like this:

   ```
   @State private var username = ""
   ```

2. Open the View Library (⌘⇧L), filter for "text", and drag it onto your Preview canvas. The code should look like this:

   ```
   TextField("Placeholder", text:Value)
   ```

3. Change the "Placeholder" text to "Username."

4. Change the second parameter (currently "Value") to be a binding to the username property like this:

   ```
   TextField("Username", text: $username)
   ```

5. Add the padding modifier with .padding(30).

6. Add a Text item below that to display the value as it's typed.

   ```
   Text(username)
   ```

7. For some other control, add the .disabled modifier. Pass in as the Bool value self.username.count == 0.

The resulting code should look like this:

```
@State private var username = ""
var body: some View {
    VStack {
        TextField("Username", text: $username)
                .padding(30)
```

```
Text("Hello, Swift")
    .font(.largeTitle)
    .fontWeight(.bold)
    .foregroundColor(Color.blue)
    .padding(30.0)
    .frame(width: 200.0, height:400.0)
    .background(Color.green)
    .cornerRadius(40.0)

Button(action: {
    print ("tapped!")
    self.isReady.toggle()
}, label: { Text("Tap Me") })
    .disabled(self.username.count == 0)
```

To run the app in Live Preview, tap the play button in the icon bar above the UI in the Canvas (Figure 3-14).

Figure 3-14. *Button Bar in the Canvas*

If you followed the steps, you should be able to type in the TextField and see the same value in the Text item below it (Figure 3-15).

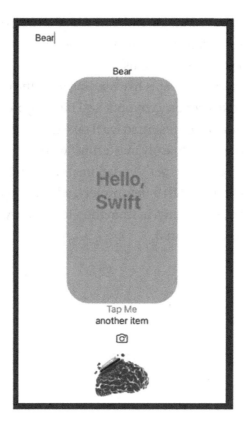

Figure 3-15. *Ending UI for the Exercise*

Also, the Tap Me button should only be enabled when there is text in the TextField.

Chapter Summary

Each of the controls we've explored in this chapter is very common in SwiftUI development. It's important to be familiar with what they are and their modifiers.

We'll see as we cover more ground how some controls can be combined and have overlap and what other modifiers, gestures, events, and more that we have provided for us.

We'll also cover more concepts like binding from the Combine framework. The @State property wrapper and binding are a small piece of that. It can be new and confusing so we'll take it slow. But it is also very powerful and a key concept to truly mastering SwiftUI.

I want to encourage you to get some more practice with everything we've done in this chapter. Start a new project, add various UI elements, explore the modifiers, drop items in from the View Library, and generally practice with what we've covered.

CHAPTER 4

Binding Source of Truth

We introduced @State in the previous chapter. We'll revisit that briefly here as well as discuss more concepts of the flow of data in SwiftUI.

Data Drives the UI

Typically, in app development, the UI represents the data and state. When the user taps a button or flips a switch, the event drives a method call. In that method, we typically have code that updates the current data.

In the last chapter, we looked at how we used @State to specify the source of truth for the toggle switch. By binding the isReady boolean variable to the toggle, we saw that toggling the switch updated the value. This was evident by the label updating its text.

But also changing the source of truth value, isReady, caused a new rendering of the UI. This included the toggle to reflect the new boolean value from the source of truth.

Binding this source of truth (value) to the UI keeps both in sync automatically via the Property Wrapper.

© Bear Cahill 2021
B. Cahill, *UI Design for iOS App Development*,
https://doi.org/10.1007/978-1-4842-6449-2_4

Flow Steps

The process stated earlier has a few steps. The steps are mostly behind the scenes for the user and the developer.

Let's take a quick look again at the code for the state variable and the binding:

```
@State private var isReady = false

Toggle(isOn: $isReady,
       label: {
        Text("Ready: " + (isReady ? "Yes" : "No"))
})
```

The isReady variable is the source of truth for the Toggle. When it changes, the UI will be rendered again. That causes the toggle to update as well as the Text label.

The steps in that process are

1. User action – Tap on the toggle.

2. Value update – isReady toggled.

3. View update – Toggle and Text change.

4. UI displayed – The UI renders on the screen.

Whenever a bound property changes, the UI will render on the screen with the updates. The framework manages the dependency.

Let's take a look at using a Stepper. A Stepper can take multiple closures – one to handle when the user taps the minus sign (–) for decrement and one for the plus (+) for increment. Here's an example of decrementing and incrementing a property with the Stepper (Figure 4-1).

```
struct ContentView: View {
    @State private var counter : Int = 0
    var body: some View {
        VStack {
            Stepper(onIncrement: {
                self.counter += 1
            }, onDecrement: {
                self.counter -= 1
            }) {
                Text.init("\(counter)")
                    .padding(10)
            }
            .padding(100)
        }

    }
}
```

Figure 4-1. *Stepper Code*

In this example, we have a Stepper and a label displaying the current count. Since the Stepper is the only UI element, it doesn't need to be within a VStack. Chances are some form of stack will be necessary at some point assuming there will be more UI elements. The app, when run, looks like Figure 4-2.

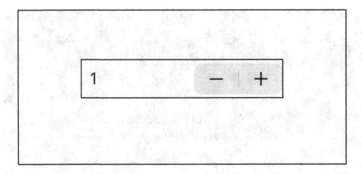

Figure 4-2. *Stepper UI*

But instead of writing the value changes in closures, we can bind the counter property to the Stepper.

COUNTER UPDATE IN THE UI

In this exercise, we'll add code to bind an @State property to the Stepper. This will use a different initializer. The initializer we want takes the value to bind.

1. Open a project (existing or new) and click the ContentView.swift file for editing. We want to start with an empty ContentView body definition.

2. Create a Stepper instance and notice the options for code completion (Figure 4-3).

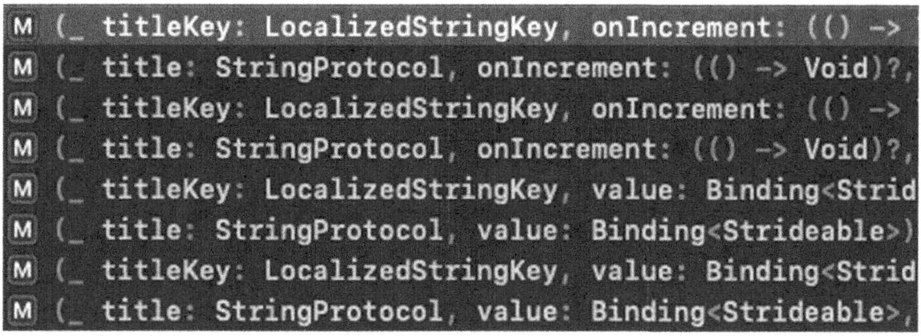

```
M  (_ titleKey: LocalizedStringKey, onIncrement: (() ->
M  (_ title: StringProtocol, onIncrement: (() -> Void)?,
M  (_ titleKey: LocalizedStringKey, onIncrement: (() ->
M  (_ title: StringProtocol, onIncrement: (() -> Void)?,
M  (_ titleKey: LocalizedStringKey, value: Binding<Strid
M  (_ title: StringProtocol, value: Binding<Strideable>)
M  (_ titleKey: LocalizedStringKey, value: Binding<Strid
M  (_ title: StringProtocol, value: Binding<Strideable>,
```

Figure 4-3. *Stepper Initializers*

The previous example used the first initializer. It takes the two closures and a label parameter. This time, we'll use the initializer that takes a StringProtocol type, a value, and a range. The range is a closed range of numbers for the Stepper's value.

The code looks like this:

```
Stepper("\(counter)", value: $counter, in: 0...9)
```

This code does a few things for us:

1. It displays the current counter value next to the Stepper.

2. It binds the counter as the source of truth to the Stepper's value.

3. It limits the Stepper's values to zero through nine.

The UI will look nearly identical to what it was before. The functionality is the same as well. However, we are no longer using a functionality in our code to keep the counter value current.

The framework is doing the work for us to update the state and render the changes in the UI.

Strideable

You may have noticed that the value parameter of the initializer takes a type of Binding. That's the property wrapper for the @State value that is managed by the framework for us.

Binding is a struct that wraps the value. The wrapped value must conform to the Strideable protocol. Strideable extends the Comparable protocol which extends the Equatable protocol.

So the value property much implements all of these:

- == (Equatable)

- < (Comparable)

- <= (Comparable)

- > (Comparable)

- >= (Comparable)

- distance (to other : Self) -> Self.Stride

- advanced (by n: Self.Stride) -> Self

The equal-equal and comparison operators are pretty straightforward. The distance and advanced functions are from the Strideable protocol.

The distance function takes a value of the same type as the @State bound variable (e.g., Int in our case) and returns the "distance" from another value. Int is Strideable so 5.distance(to: 100) returns 95.

Strideable has an associatedType of Stride which is defined as something that implements Comparable and SignedNumeric. So returning Self.Stride from distance will be a number. For the Strideable implementation of Int, the Stride type is also an Int:

```
public typealias Stride = Int
```

The advanced function returns the same type as what value it's called on (e.g., calling advanced on an Int returns an Int). It takes a Self.Stride which is defined by that type as well. So for an Int, calling advanced requires an Int passed in and returns an Int advanced by that value. So 5.advanced(by: 5) returns 10.

Our counter property is an Int which implements all of these and works perfectly for our value parameter. Other Swift numeric types such as Double, Float, and Decimal also implement Strideable.

Other controls use binding as well, but the type Binding wraps may be another type. For example, Textfield takes a Binding that wraps a String. There's a type we know about!

Property Wrapper

The @State property wrapper is the Binding type. If you drill into its definition, you'll see it's a struct with the generic Value which it wraps. Like an optional, there are various initializers, functions, and extensions defined.

However, as we will allow the framework to manage the memory and handling of the property wrapper, we won't often need to do anything other than bind it. The system will handle it from there for wrapping and unwrapping the value. We can set the value (or let the UI element do it), and the rest is taken care of.

@Binding

Another directive for binding is @Binding. This allows you to specify a property in another object to be bound to something passed in.

We may want to take a UI element(s) and put them in a separate struct. This can be reused throughout our code. But we may want the value to be bound based on what is using our new element.

For example, if we want our stepper control as we designed it in the exercise, we can do that. We just need a new struct that implements View and have our Stepper control in it like Figure 4-4.

```
struct MyStepper : View {
    @State private var counter : Int = 0
    var body: some View {
        Stepper("\(counter)", value: $counter,
                in: 0...9)
        .padding(100)
    }
}
```

Figure 4-4. *MyStepper Struct*

Here, we have a new struct called MyStepper. It can be in the same file or another file. In our original ContentView, we can include this in the UI with MyStepper() in place of the Stepper code we had.

You can have any number of these View types included in your code just like a Button, Text, or anything else. It's good for cleaner, more maintainable code. And it's great for reuse.

However, in Figure 4-4, we have the counter as a local property. What we really want is to be able to base the counter on an external source of truth.

Using @State is good for within a given struct. In this case, the source of truth is outside the MyStepper implementation. For that, we use the @Binding directive.

So we replace the @State with @Binding, and this

```
@State private var counter : Int = 0
```

becomes this:

```
@Binding var counter : Int
```

We do not need to provide a default value because it will now be passed in during the creation of MyStepper. Notice it is no longer private as it needs to be externally accessed. Structs in Swift get an automatically generated member-wise initializer. In our case, that is the counter value. So the code complete for creating our MyStepper looks like Figure 4-5.

Figure 4-5. *MyStepper Initializer with the counter Parameter*

The type for the property is a Binding (property wrapper) for an Int. Like with Optionals, we can pass in the type (Int) directly. For our code, that can be the original counter property like this:

```
MyStepper(counter: $counter)
```

Now our counter property is passed into MyStepper as a property wrapper and managed for us. Changing the value via MyStepper updates our local counter property.

What if we needed two steppers? We can add a second MyStepper exactly like we added the first one.

If we bind counter to both, what will happen? Try it out. Note: Use a VStack or similar to group the MyStepper instances.

```
MyStepper(counter: $counter)
MyStepper(counter: $counter)
```

Since both instances of MyStepper have the same value, they both update the same source of truth. Updating one will change the value for the other. The UI rendering will reflect these changes like Figure 4-6.

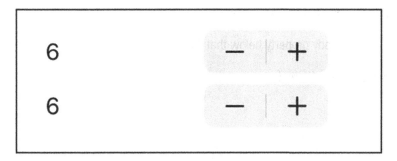

Figure 4-6. *MyStepper Instances with the Same Binding*

I changed the padding to only be horizontal so that they are closer together. But otherwise the UI is expected: two MySteppers in sync with the same binding.

What about binding for a Textfield? As mentioned earlier, Textfield uses a String as opposed to a number. Is that different? Not on the surface and not in practice. Instead of the parameter type of Binding<Strideable>, it will be Binding<String>.

Let's try creating another View type with a Textfield and binding from the ContentView.

TEXTFIELD INPUT STRUCT

In this exercise, we're going to add a TextField to our UI. We will create another struct (in the same file or another file) called MyTextInput. It needs a textfield and a property for binding.

Create a new struct (in the same file or another one) named MyInput like this:

```
struct MyInput : View {
}
```

It needs to have two things: the body computed property and a property for binding when it's created.

Add the binding property just below the struct line like this:

```
@Binding var stringVal : String
```

Now start the body property below that like this:

```
var body: some View {
}
```

Flesh out the body property with a Textfield element using at least the title and binding like this:

```
TextField("Enter Value:",
          text: $stringVal,
          onEditingChanged: { (changed) in
          print(changed)
}) {
    print("commit: \(self.stringVal)")
}
```

Notice there are several initializers to choose from. This includes some with closures for when the editing changes (start editing and end editing). This onEditingChanged closure takes a Bool where true means the value is currently being edited, and false means it ended.

Another closure is called onCommit which is called when the user taps the return key.

Optionally add some padding to the element to match your MyStepper appearance.

```
.padding(.horizontal, 100)
```

Add a String property in your ContentView that you'll bind to the MyInput.

```
@State private var username = ""
```

Add the MyInput with the String property item to your UI below the MyStepper.

```
MyInput(stringVal: $username)
```

Add a Text item displaying the String property below the MyInput item in the UI.

```
Text(username)
```

The code (not including the MyStepper) should look similar to Figure 4-7.

```
struct MyInput : View {
    @Binding var stringVal : String
    var body: some View {
        TextField("Enter Value:",
                  text: $stringVal,
                  onEditingChanged: { (changed) in
                      print (changed)
        }) {
            print ("commit: \(self.stringVal)")
        }
        .padding(.horizontal, 100)
    }
}


struct ContentView: View {
    @State private var counter : Int = 0
    @State private var username = ""

    var body: some View {
        VStack {
            MyStepper(counter: $counter)
            MyInput(stringVal: $username)|
            Text(username)
        }
```

Figure 4-7. *MyInput Struct and Updated ContentView Body*

The UI should look something like Figure 4-8 with the text from the Textfield displayed in the Text label.

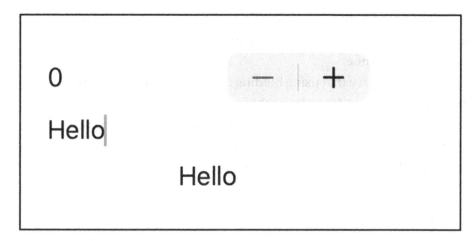

Figure 4-8. *UI with MyStepper, MyInput, and Text*

We see that additional UI elements can be created with binding from the items creating them. Of course, we could bind multiple items to the same UI element we create.

Chapter Summary

In this chapter, we reviewed the concept of using @State for property wrappers in a given struct. Using the built-in UI elements to manage and sync values saves coding and avoids bugs with data not being synced.

We also got an understanding of how binding numeric types works with the Binding struct and its Strideable and Stride types. We also used binding of a String for a Textfield.

@State and @Binding help keep the values stored in a single source of truth. No need to copy, update, or sync values. As the user updates their input, the values get updated, the UI gets recreated, and the rendering shows the new state.

Allowing the framework to do this work for us creates less coding time and less code. It's also more maintainable and benefits to updates in the framework over time.

I hope you agree that using binding in these ways is a great start to simplifying the UI and its relationship to values they relate to.

We'll be building on these concepts going forward. I encourage you to practice what we've done and explore more options. Try other UI elements like Slider, Button, Toggle, Image, and more.

CHAPTER 5

ObservableObjects

In the previous chapters, we've used isolated properties for values. But in development we usually have more complex models. We typically deal with structs or classes that have multiple properties representing our data.

In this chapter, we'll look at how to observe property updates of reference type objects. When the properties change, the UI will be notified and updated.

To accomplish this, we'll use aspects of the Combine framework. We'll go into more detail of that framework in a later chapter. For now, we'll see how it works for our purposes of binding.

We will continue to work in our same SUINotes project. We'll be adding some new objects in our existing code. For the ContentView struct, we'll remove the current properties and body implementation and start fresh.

Typical Model

We are all familiar with structs and classes. Here's a typical class representing a note object:

```
enum Priority : Int {
    case low, medium, high
}
```

© Bear Cahill 2021
B. Cahill, *UI Design for iOS App Development*,
https://doi.org/10.1007/978-1-4842-6449-2_5

```
class Note {
    var text = ""
    var updateAtTime = Date()
    var priority = Priority.medium
}
```

Here, we have a Note class with three properties of types String, Date, and Priority. Priority is defined as an enumeration for low, medium, and high. It also has an underlying type of Int so low, medium, and high map to 0, 1, and 2, respectively. This will help when doing comparisons of the priority values.

Also, Note has default values for all of the properties so we don't need a defined initializer.

We want to display the note objects' contents on the UI so we need an instance of one. Since the Note class contains a Date property, we'll also create a DateFormatter.

Here's how our ContentView struct properties look in ContentView. swift after we remove any previous properties:

```
struct ContentView: View {
    var note = Note()
    var df = DateFormatter()
    ...
```

But we need to set up the styles for our df instance. To do that, we'll create an initializer for our ContentView. It looks like this:

```
init() {
    df.dateStyle = .none
    df.timeStyle = .medium
    note.text = "Note Text"
}
```

Notice I also set the note.text property to have a nonempty string value. This is so there's something to display in the UI.

Displaying the contents of our Note instance is pretty straightforward. We can use two Text items to show the text and createdAt properties. The DateFormatter will give us a nice looking String for our Date.

BUILD THE NOTE UI

In this exercise, we're going to build the UI to display the model as we have it defined. This includes two Text items to start.

1. Define the Priority enumeration and Note class as it's presented earlier, if you haven't already.

2. Replace the body implementation with two Text items in a VStack: one for the text and one for the updatedAtTime.

   Here's what it looks like:

```
var body: some View {
    VStack {
        Text(note.text)
        Text(df.string(from: note.updatedAtTime))
    }
}
```

   For the priority, we want something a bit more visual than text. Let's use star images. SF Symbols has a variety of options for this. We'll use the star.circle image.

3. Add an HStack for the star.circle images for priority:

```
HStack {
    Image(systemName: "star.circle")
    Image(systemName: note.priority.rawValue > 0
        ? "star.circle" : "circle")
```

65

```
        Image(systemName: note.priority.rawValue > 1
            ? "star.circle" : "circle")
    }
```

4. Run the app (⌘+r) and verify the UI looks as it should.

For our note with a default priority of .medium, the UI will look like Figure 5-1.

Figure 5-1. *Note UI*

Feel free to play with the UI to have it display differently. This will be the bases
for moving forward to have the UI update when our model changes.

If the note changes, we want to display the changes. That might be the
text, date, or priority. We'll add observers to the text and priority properties
on Note:

```
class Note : ObservableObject {
    var text = "" {
        didSet {
            self.updatedAtTime = Date()
        }
    }
    var updatedAtTime = Date()
    var priority = Priority.medium {
```

```
    didSet {
        self.updatedAtTime = Date()
    }
  }
}
```

Whenever the text or priority is changed, the updatedAtTime is also updated.

Let's add a button to update the text of the note:

```
Button(action: {
    let newTime = self.df.string(from:Date())
    self.note.text = "now \(newTime)"
    print(self.note.text)
}) {
    Text("Update")
}
```

The UI looks like Figure 5-2 now.

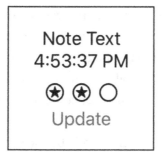

Figure 5-2. *Note UI with an Update Button*

I'm also printing out the new text value to verify it's getting updated.

If we run this, we'll see the printout shows the updatedAtTime is set to the current time (e.g., "now 4:53:39 PM"), but the UI doesn't update. Why not?

Binding?

You may be thinking it's because there's no binding to the value. That's true. However, unlike with a Toggle or similar, ContentView doesn't have a value it needs to pass along. More than that, the Note could be created by some other object and passed into ContentView.

If you're dealing with an existing code base, the model may already be defined and implemented. We don't want to start requiring classes become structs, some values have @Binding and are passed in, maybe new initializers, and so on.

No, instead we want to make as few changes to the model as possible.

Observing Reference Objects

This is where the Combine framework comes up. We'll spend more time with it later. For now, we just need to understand that it can be used to publish updates.

This is great when you have **reference types** that could be passed around all over your code. It may be changed at any point outside of your knowledge. But by using an ObservableObject, your UI can stay up to date.

When we looked at State/Binding, the source of truth was in our ContentView. We passed that value to another object using a Property Wrapper. Changes were made in other code, but the source of truth was still the source and was updated.

For binding objects, it will effectively be the other way around. The object in question is the source of truth, and we want to know when something changes. How?

The ObservableObject protocol is the answer. In our case, that's the Note class – hence part of the reason we're using a class object for the Note. It needs to be a reference type.

ObservableObject Protocol

The ObservableObject protocol inherits from the AnyObject protocol. That means it can only be implemented by a class (not a struct or enumeration).

So let's declare that our Note class conforms to ObservableObject. First, we need to import the Combine framework at the top with

```
import Combine
```

Then we'll update our Note class code like this:

```
class Note : ObservableObject {...
```

Notice that you don't get any warnings or errors. That's always good. There's nothing in ObservableObject that is required that doesn't also provide a default implementation.

The changes to Note need to be published, and there's a default publisher created for us!

We do have to make a change to the note property in our ContentView as well. We'll use another property wrapper here like we did with State and Binding. It's called ObservedObject, and we need to add it to our note like this:

```
@ObservedObject var note = Note()
```

We've told the compiler that our Note class can be observed. Of course, nothing is required to observe it. Our ContentView wants to observe it, and it declared it so. There's only one piece left.

Publishing Updates

There are two easy ways to receive updates to values changed on an ObservedObject. And both ways are controlled by the object implementing the ObservableObject.

This means that the ObservableObject is in control of what is published and when it is published.

In our case, we are most concerned with changes to the text property on Note. I mentioned that ObservableObject has default implementations for its required pieces. One is a publisher, and the property name is objectWillChange.

Using this default publisher, we can send out the new values whenever something changes. We already have a didSet observer on the text property in Note. That's a great place to publish the change. The code looks like this:

```
var text = "" {
    didSet {
        self.updatedAtTime = Date()
        self.objectWillChange.send()
    }
}
```

Now when we tap the Update button, the textfields for the text and updatedAtTime are both updated. The update looks like Figure 5-3.

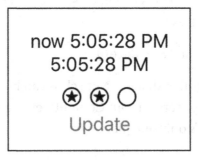

Figure 5-3. *Note UI with Updates*

Calling .send on the publisher is certainly an easy way to send out the updates. And it's particularly great when you don't want to publish changes except for key times. Maybe you want to wait until something specific happens like a write to the database and then publish the values.

You may have a class that only publishes updates at certain time intervals. Maybe you only want to publish when a threshold is set on a property or other criteria are met. In those cases, the .send call on the publisher is very useful.

In our case, we want the new text value published whenever it's set. Calling .send in the didSet observer works great for that. Another way to do it for all changes to a property is the @Published attribute.

@Published

The @Published attribute on a property creates a publisher of that type. We can add that attribute to our text property in Note. Also, we can now remove our call to .send in the didSet observer.

The result will be the same in our case. Tapping the Update button in the UI will update the text which will then be published, and the UI is updated.

The code now looks like this:

```
@Published var text = "" {
    didSet {
        self.updatedAtTime = Date()
    }
}
```

We may also want to add @Published to other properties. In our case, it makes sense to publish the priority. It might make the most sense to publish the updatedAtTime. In that case, if we wrote our code well, anytime the object is updated, it will publish.

Let's try something else.

TIMER TO CHANGE PRIORITY

Let's change our Note class to automatically create the priority after a certain amount of time. We'll add an init to the Note with a Timer. When it fires, it will level up the priority by one level each time.

1. Change the default priority of a Note to .low:

    ```
    var priority = Priority.low {...
    ```

2. Add an initializer to the Note class:

    ```
    init() {
    }
    ```

3. Add a Timer in the init to fire every X seconds (e.g., 10) and to repeat. The body of the Timer's closure should set the priority up a level.

    ```
    Timer.scheduledTimer(withTimeInterval: 10.0,
                            repeats: true) { (timer) in
        self.priority = Priority(rawValue:
            self.priority.rawValue + 1) ??
            Priority.high
        if self.priority == .high {
            timer.invalidate()
        }
    }
    ```

Every 10 seconds, the timer will fire. It will create a new priority based on the current priority's raw value + 1. If that number is too high, it defaults to Priority.high.

If the priority is set to .high, it will invalidate the timer. We may want to keep the timer going in case the user sets the priority back to a lower setting. We don't have that in our current UI so there's no need.

4. Run the app and verify it increases the priority every
   10 seconds until it's high.

The first and last results should look like Figure 5-4.

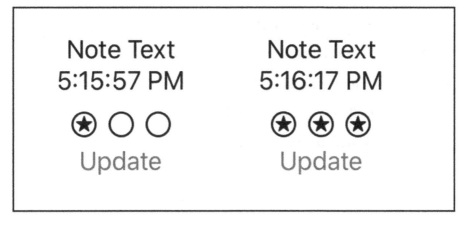

Figure 5-4. *Auto-updating UI: First and Last States*

From this exercise, we see that whether changes happen via user interaction
or otherwise, the changes are published.

Chapter Summary

Using the ObservableObject protocol allows for reference type objects to
publish their changes. You can take new or existing model classes and have
them implement ObservableObject with a few small changes.

That makes the changes to existing code very minor. If you've ever
added the Codable protocol to legacy code, you know about how easy it
can be.

For code that is interested in the updates, the additions are also small.
It can be as little as adding the @ObservedObject attribute to a property.

We introduced some complex concepts in this chapter with the Combine. While a lot is going on behind the scenes, there were only a few steps we need to do:

1. Import Combine.

2. Add @ObservableObject to Note.

3. Add @ObservedObject to the note property.

4. Decide if we wanted to either

    1. Call .send on the publisher or

    2. Add @Published to a property

CHAPTER 6

Environment Values

So far, we've seen how to use the State property wrapper for values within a given view. We've also seen how to bind local values to external variables with Binding.

In both of those cases, our code needs to create and control the values. These values, via property wrappers, are then passed around. Using property wrappers in this way keeps the source of truth both isolated and always in sync.

But what about values that might be created somewhere else? What about values that might affect the whole app or device?

SwiftUI has solutions for that as well with Environment values and objects.

Environment Values

Getting various environment values is easy with SwiftUI. And if your UI is based on them, changes will invalidate the current view. That means a new one is created and rendered for the user. Put that all together, and it means changes to values used in your UI will cause the necessary update.

SwiftUI provides a good list of values to access from the Environment. These values include areas such as accessibility settings, color scheme, control attributes, and even CoreData.

You can see all of the available variables from SwiftUI here: `https://developer.apple.com/documentation/swiftui/environmentvalues`.

© Bear Cahill 2021
B. Cahill, *UI Design for iOS App Development*,
https://doi.org/10.1007/978-1-4842-6449-2_6

Let's look at color scheme as a simple example. To access the value in our code, we need to use the @Environment property wrapper for a variable. We specify the key path of the specific value we want. The code looks like this:

```
@Environment(\.colorScheme) var lightOrDark
```

Now we have the color scheme value stored in a property named lightOrDark. In our UI, we can adapt our UI based on this value. Then, if the value changes, our UI will be updated.

Let's say we want a button title, "Update," to be blue normally but green in dark mode. We can now use the value of lightOrDark to determine that.

Using our previous chapter project, I'll use lightOrDark to set the accent color.

```
Text ("Update")
    .accentColor(lightOrDark == .light ?
        .blue : .green)
```

When run in the simulator, if dark mode is off, the UI will include the button with a blue title. If we switch to dark mode (⇧⌘A) using a simulator/device that supports dark mode, the button will switch to green like in Figure 6-1.

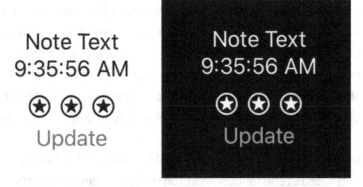

Figure 6-1. *UI Updated to Dark Mode*

Our Text items are created with default settings. By default, it uses the system label color. That varies depending on the dark mode setting. If you inspect or print out the UIColor.label.cgColor, it will also vary depending on the current dark mode setting.

Those two Text items are updated for us. The same is true for the button text item. So, by default, these items will update based on the dark mode setting. Or we can handle it in a custom fashion as in the preceding code.

Settings Per View

Each view inherits the Environment settings from its parent. However, you can override these settings when creating a view.

Our Button has a Text item for the title. In the previous section, we're setting the color of that title based on the lightOrDark value. For our whole (small) app right now, we're using all the same settings for the Environment.

When our ContentView is created, the Environment is inherited and is propagated through all of its views: Text, Button, and so on. But we can change that. We can modify the Environment when a view is created.

To modify the Environment, we use the .environment modifier on the return of the view creation. Let's say we want to force our top Text item to always be in dark mode. Of course, when the background is white, the white text won't be visible so I'll also add a background modifier for gray.

```
Text(note.text)
    .environment(\.colorScheme, .dark)
    .background(Color.gray)
```

I use the .environment modifier to specify the key path of the color scheme and a value (i.e., .dark). The other value option for this enumeration is .light. Now the UI forces dark mode on this Text. Running the app and switching to dark mode looks like Figure 6-2.

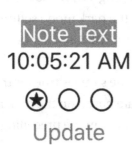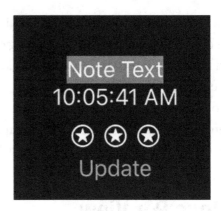

Figure 6-2. *UI Updated to Dark Mode*

Using method chaining, we can call both the .environment and .background modifiers. Similarly, we could call multiple .environment modifiers and change various values.

These changes will then be inherited to any and all views created by that view. In our case, it may seem like that doesn't apply. However, we don't have any control of the Text and can't know what it's creating. If we look at a view hierarchy rendering (Debug ➤ View Debugging... ➤ Capture View Hierarchy) like Figure 6-3, we see there may be more to a Text item than we thought.

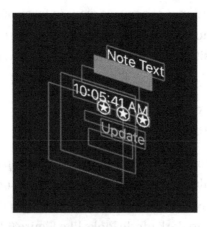

Figure 6-3. *3D Rendering of UI*

A good thing to learn here is that the appearance may be more complicated than it seems. So while just setting one value (e.g., accentColor) may seem to do the trick, you should consider what the core change should be (e.g., colorScheme).

Earlier, we looked at passing environment settings into a Text element. We can do the same if we first pull out a part of our UI into a separate struct.

NOTE VIEW WITH ENVIRONMENT

In this exercise, we're going to pull out the UI items that display the Note. We'll put them into a new View and have that struct control displaying the note details.

However, we want the creating element (i.e., ContentView in our app) to control the environment. Other than the Note instance and the .environment modifier, we don't want ContentView to control other aspects of the UI for the newly created NoteView.

In light (left) and dark (right) modes, we want the interface to look like Figure 6-4.

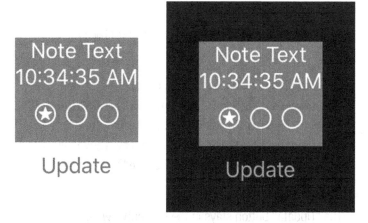

Figure 6-4. *NoteView in Light (Left) and Dark (Right) Modes*

Feel free to try to tackle this before looking at the following steps and code. In short, you need to put the Note-related UI elements in a new NoteView struct that conforms to the View protocol. Keep the .environment modifier separate and call it on the newly created NoteView element.

1. Create a new struct called NoteView that conforms to the View:

```
struct NoteView : View {
}
```

2. Add a body computed property to the NoteView with a VStack:

```
var body: some View {
    VStack {
    }
}
```

3. At the bottom of the VStack, add the .background modifier:

```
}.background(Color.gray)
```

4. Cut and paste the two Text elements and the HStack of Image items from the ContentView body into the VStack of the NoteView:

```
Text(note.text)
Text(df.string(from: note.updatedAtTime))

HStack {
    Image(systemName: "star.circle")
    Image(systemName: note.priority.rawValue > 0
        ? "star.circle" : "circle")
    Image(systemName: note.priority.rawValue > 1
        ? "star.circle" : "circle")
}
```

The "Update" button stays in the ContentView body.

5. Add a Note property to the NoteView:

```
var note : Note
```

This property will be passed in so do not set it equal to anything.

6. Similarly, add a DateFormatter property which will be passed in:

```
var df : DateFormatter
```

The NoteView struct is defined and ready to be used (Figure 6-5). It has the two properties of Note and DateFormatter. We have those in our ContentView. Those are the two values in the ContentView we'll use to create our NoteView.

```swift
struct NoteView : View {
    var note : Note
    var df : DateFormatter

    var body: some View {
        VStack {
            Text(note.text)
            Text(df.string(from: note.updatedAtTime))

            HStack {
                Image(systemName: "star.circle")
                Image(systemName: note.priority.rawValue > 0
                    ? "star.circle" : "circle")
                Image(systemName: note.priority.rawValue > 1
                    ? "star.circle" : "circle")
            }
        }.background(Color.gray)
    }
}
```

Figure 6-5. *NoteView with Properties and UI Items Moved from ContentView's VStack*

7. In ContentView's body property, create a new NoteView
    instance. It should go where you previously had the two Text
    items and HStack of Images in the body of the NoteView (just
    above the Button):

    ```
    NoteView(note: self.note, df: df)
    ```

    Now we have our own UI element defined. We can pass in environment
    settings to our NoteView as we have done previously to Text.

8. Add the same .environment modifier you had before on the Text
    item now to the NoteView. Steps 7 and 8 combined look like this:

    ```
    NoteView(note: self.note, df: df)
        .environment(\.colorScheme, .dark)
    ```

9. Update the preview in the Canvas for NoteView, and it should
    look like Figure 6-6.

Figure 6-6. *NoteView UI*

Basically, this is what we want. We've shown that we can create a
NoteView to control itself while having the parent view control the
environment.

However, there are two problems. The padding isn't very appealing on the bottom. Also, if you ran it in the simulator, you may have noticed the priority stars aren't updating anymore.

Both of these issues are easily fixed. For the padding, we can still control the UI in the NoteView with a .padding modifier. If we put padding on the VStack in NoteView, it will have a bottom space that's white. That's because the padding is outside of the views. Not what we want.

Instead, if we put the padding on the last UI item (i.e., the HStack as in the following code), it will look correct:

```
HStack {
    Image(systemName: "star.circle")
    Image(systemName: note.priority.rawValue > 0
        ? "star.circle" : "circle")
    Image(systemName: note.priority.rawValue > 1
        ? "star.circle" : "circle")
}

.padding(.bottom)
```

For making the Note's priority update, we need to use the same Note instance in the UI as we created in the ContentView. We can use the ObservedObject property wrapper in the NoteView.

10. Add an ObservedObject in the NoteView:

```
@ObservedObject var note : Note
```

Since we now have the NoteView controlling the UI for updates to the note instance, we can remove the @ObservedObject from our ContentView property.

```
struct ContentView: View {
    var note = Note()
```

Once we create the Note (above) and pass it into the NoteView, changes will be published to NoteView instead of ContentView.

11. Run the app again and verify the priority stars are updated as in Figure 6-7.

Figure 6-7. *NoteView with Priority Updates*

The dark mode changes are handled as well as in Figure 6-8. Be sure you're using a simulator/device that supports dark mode.

Figure 6-8. *NoteView UI in Dark Mode*

Bonus: For extra practice, add another .environment modifier after the colorScheme setting. Try using the \.font key path and set the font for the NoteView's environment. You can set it to something like

```
Font.system(.largeTitle)
```

In this exercise, we saw that we can allow a given View to control its own UI. But we can also control the environment from the parent via the .environment modifier.

App Environment

Just like we called the .environment modifier when we created the NoteView, we can do it in other places. In the SUINotesApp.swift file created for you by the templates (named based on our project name), our ContentView is created for running the app in the simulator/device (as opposed to the Canvas).

Just like where we created our NoteView, we can set some environment settings for our ContentView. So if we wanted our app to run in dark mode, have a set font, or have a set truncation mode or various other settings, we can do it in that one place.

But remember, this means you are setting the environment for that view and its children. If you set the colorScheme to dark (or light) and the system is in light (or dark), you're only changing it for your ContentView and its children – not for the whole device. But your app would always run in dark mode despite the device settings by the user.

Or, on your ContentView instance, you can set things like the Font which will propagate:

```
ContentView()
    .environment(\.font, Font.system(.largeTitle))
```

If you create the ContentView like this in the ContentView_Previews code, your preview will use this setting in the Canvas.

If you do this in the SUINotesApp.swift file's creation of ContentView, it will use those settings when run in the simulator or device.

EnvironmentObject Property Wrapper

Sometimes, the object you want to monitor for changes doesn't come directly from the parent. It might be a bad design to pass it down through various views to get to the final view you're interested in.

In our app, the Note instance is created in the ContentView, but that might not be the best or right place. Maybe we have a model that is managed somewhere else. ContentView may have no business handling it much less creating it.

In that case, we can use the @EnvironmentObject property wrapper on the Note in NoteView. Our NoteView can ask for the Note instance just like before. ContentView is out of the mix as far as Note goes.

This means we can remove the note property from our ContentView. Further, we need to remove all references to it from the ContentView struct code. Our ContentView is getting pretty lean at this point as in Figure 6-9.

```
struct ContentView: View {
    @Environment(\.colorScheme) var lightOrDark
    var df = DateFormatter()

    init() {
        df.dateStyle = .none
        df.timeStyle = .medium
    }

    var body: some View {
        VStack {
            NoteView()
                .environment(\.colorScheme, .dark)
        }
    }
}
```

Figure 6-9. *ContentView Code Without Note*

Similarly, we could move the DateFormatter into NoteView (below), and ContentView gets even leaner as in Figure 6-10. If you had added the lightOrDark property, you can remove that too.

```
struct ContentView: View {
    var body: some View {
        VStack {
            NoteView()
                .environment(\.colorScheme, .dark)
        }
    }
}
```

Figure 6-10. *ContentView Code Without DateFormatter*

87

Our NoteView gets a bit heftier with the DateFormatter, but that may be where it belongs depending on the requirements (see Figure 6-11). Without the note passed into the NoteView creation nor the initializer setting it, we have an error. We'll fix that by changing the property wrapper and, by doing that, the way the note property is set.

```
struct NoteView : View {
    @ObservedObject var note : Note
    var df = DateFormatter()

    init() {
        self.df.timeStyle = .medium
        self.df.dateFormat = .none
    }                                        ⊗  Return from initializer without initializing all stored properties

    var body: some View {
        VStack {
            Text(note.text)
            Text(df.string(from: note.updatedAtTime))

            HStack {
                Image(systemName: "star.circle")
                Image(systemName: note.priority.rawValue > 0
                    ? "star.circle" : "circle")
                Image(systemName: note.priority.rawValue > 1
                    ? "star.circle" : "circle")
            }
            .padding(.bottom)
        }.background(Color.gray)
    }
}
```

Figure 6-11. *NoteView with DateFormatter with Error*

ContentView has nothing to do with the model Note instance. NoteView, however, needs it, and we have a compile error due to that. This is where @EnvironmentObject comes in. We'll tell NoteView to get it from the environment.

So add the property wrapper to our note declaration:

```
@EnvironmentObject var note : Note
```

We'll discuss this in more detail in Chapter 15. The short version is since the Note struct is already defined as an ObservableObject, it's fine to declare a property of it with the @EnvironmentObject wrapper.

Now the note is taken care of in NoteView. But a Note instance is never actually set. If we run the app, it crashes with this error:

```
Fatal error: No ObservableObject of type
Note found. A View.environmentObject(_:)

for Note may be missing as an ancestor of
 this view.: file SwiftUI, line 0
```

We need to set a Note in the environment. It's no longer passed in by its creator. That means it can be defined and set in the environment anytime before the NoteView is created. It could be done in a Model management class or struct or wherever. Let's define and set it somewhere else for demonstration purposes.

We'll do it in SUINotesApp.swift with the .environmentObject modifier. First, we'll create a Note instance as a property of the SUINotesApp struct:

```
struct SUINotesApp: App {

    var note : Note {
        let aNote = Note()
        aNote.text = "SUINotesApp.swift"
        return aNote
    }
```

In the body property's WindowGroup, we'll create our ContentView as before but add the .environmentObject call for the Note instance:

```
ContentView()
    .environment(\.font,
                Font.system(.largeTitle))
        .environmentObject(note)
```

If we run the app in the simulator or device (not the Canvas preview), it now uses this note from the environment. Since we're doing this in the SUINotesApp struct, these changes don't affect the preview in the Canvas. To do that, we'd need similar code in the CodeView_Previews which we'll do in the next section.

The updates (e.g., priority stars) still get propagated to the UI like in Figure 6-12.

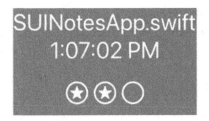

Figure 6-12. UI Using Note from the Environment

Did you notice anything sneaky about this? We just set a Note in the environment, and NoteView got it. No key value. No accessor. It just got the one we wanted.

Remember the error message we got earlier? It said "No ObservableObject of type Note found." It's looking for it "by type." So when NoteView is created, it gets the (one and only) item of type Note.

So if we replace it later or run the .environmentObject modifier in ContentView to override the normally inherited environment, NoteView will get that one.

If you need multiple notes, you might need to add an array, manager class, or some singleton to the environment. Or you might find that storing items in the environment isn't the right choice for what you need to do.

Preview Environment

You may have also noticed your preview quit working. Since we are creating the Note in the SUINotesApp struct now, our ContentView_ Previews isn't getting that environment setting.

We can set it in the ContentPreview previews computed property, but it's a little tricky.

For one thing, the previews property is static. If the Note instance is created outside of that, it needs to be static as well like this:

```
struct ContentView_Previews: PreviewProvider {
    static var note = Note()
    static var previews: some View {
        ContentView()
            .environmentObject(note)
    }
}
```

But since it's static, we don't have the opportunity to initialize the text property of the note. So in our case, the text item will be blank.

It could be defined as static as a computed property like this code:

```
static var note : Note {
    let note = Note()
    note.text = "Static Computed"
    return note
}
```

You can also create the instance in the .environmentObject call like this:

```
.environmentObject(Note())
```

Depending on how you want the preview to appear, you have options. Similarly, we've seen there are options about when to create something, how to pass it around or access it, what is the source of truth, and other related possibilities.

Usage

The question then comes up of when do you use which type of property wrapper and observable binding.

The @State property wrapper is best for values within a single view. If you have a counter or timer start value and you want the UI to stay in sync, @State might be just right.

@Binding is when the source of truth is somewhere else. The MyStepper view used this property wrapper to modify the source of truth outside of itself. Anything creating an instance of MyStepper needs to pass in the source of truth using the $ for binding.

@ObservedObject is for reference types (e.g., classes) that are declared to conform to the ObservableObject protocol. If you declare your property instance with the @ObservedObject wrapper, the implementation of the class now needs to be coded to publish the updates. This is done either through calls on a publisher (e.g., self.objectWillChange.send()) or by declaring the properties with @Published.

So @ObservedObject is best used when you have reference types that need to be monitored for updates to the UI. This is also a good option if you already have a reference type model in your app and you're converting to SwiftUI. It requires little change to the existing model code.

@Environment is good for getting and setting environment variables based on built-in key path constants like .colorScheme. The settings are passed down into views when created. Environment settings for views can be set via the .environment modifier on the view when created.

Environment settings are good for accessing values across your app or down paths of your app. They don't need to be specifically passed around – just inherited.

@EnvironmentObject is for declaring an object to be loaded from the environment "by type." It's vital that this value is actually set or the app will crash. Like environment settings, these values can be set on views when created and passed down through inheritance. Environment objects are set with the .environmentObject modifier.

Environment objects are good similar to environment settings. If you need access to an object in various places of your app but it doesn't make sense to pass them around all over, environment objects are a good choice.

Custom Environment Values

It's not difficult to add your own values to the environment. You need a struct that conforms to EnvironmentKey which has one required static computed property that's read only:

```
static var defaultValue: Self.Value { get }
```

When you implement that, you just need the defaultValue to return the default value. If we want to store the default value for the Note textfield, the type will be a String. So our environment key could look like this:

```
struct NoteInitialTextEnvironmentKey: EnvironmentKey{
    static var defaultValue: String = "Default Note"
}
```

In extended EnvironmentValues, we can add a computed property that uses that key to get and set our value. Whatever we name the property will be the key path we use to access it. We'll call ours defaultNoteText:

```
extension EnvironmentValues {
    var defaultNoteText: String {
    }
}
```

The key we defined here will be used in the subscript of the EnvironmentValues:

```
get {
    return
        self[NoteInitialTextEnvironmentKey.self]
}
set {
    self[NoteInitialTextEnvironmentKey.self] =
        newValue
}
```

With the preceding code defined, we can set the default Note text with the .environment modifier:

```
.environment(\.defaultNoteText, "New Default")
```

And we can retrieve the value like any other environment property:

```
@Environment(\.defaultNoteText) var defaultText
    : String
```

Or get it directly using the subscript on an EnvironmentValues instance like this:

```
EnvironmentValues()
        [NoteInitialTextEnvironmentKey.self]
```

If you're thinking that's a good bit of work to store a value in the environment when only one class may need it, I agree. In this case, a simple constant or possibly a setting in UserDefaults would be fine.

But hopefully you see how it works. Then, when it's more applicable, you'll understand how you can employ it in your code.

Now that we have a default value, our note instance has a nonempty String value when it is created. This also fixed our blank Textfield in the preview.

Chapter Summary

In this chapter, we learned about the Environment. It's a handy place to find a variety of values for the environment your app is running in. You can also set your own custom values. Watch out for the temptation to use Environment and EnvironmentValues where it's really overengineering.

We saw how settings with the .environment modifier propagate to created views down the hierarchy.

The .environmentObject modifier is useful for setting reference type objects in the environment too. Remember, these are accessed by type. There are two big effects of this fact. First, if this value isn't set in the associated environment, the app will crash. Second, the value will be replaced if set again.

SwiftUI gives us a variety of tools for accessing a value via the framework. In many cases, the framework doing the work for us is very helpful. But it's important to consider the need for the data and which mechanism is best for a given case.

CHAPTER 7

List of Items

In this chapter, we'll turn our attention back to the UI as far as visual elements go. We've seen how to add simple elements like Text and Button. Now we'll look at listing items.

If you've used UIKit in the past, you're undoubtedly familiar with UITableView and its assortment of relatives: UITableViewController, UITableViewDataSource, UITableViewDelegate, and UITableViewCell.

In SwiftUI, we'll use a List in place of the UITableView. For the rows, we'll use Views just like we have been using. Doesn't that sound much more simple? No prototype cells. No back and forth of the table asking for a cell and your code asking for a dequeued cell and the height of the cell returned somewhere else.

List

Creating a visual list of items will feel more like a loop than creating a UI. That's because it will loop over the values you tell it to. Each iteration of the loop will create a View to be displayed.

Let's start with a simple example in a new iOS app project. Create your project with options for SwiftUI for the interface and SwiftUI App for the life cycle. Your ContentView code should look like Figure 7-1.

© Bear Cahill 2021
B. Cahill, *UI Design for iOS App Development*,
https://doi.org/10.1007/978-1-4842-6449-2_7

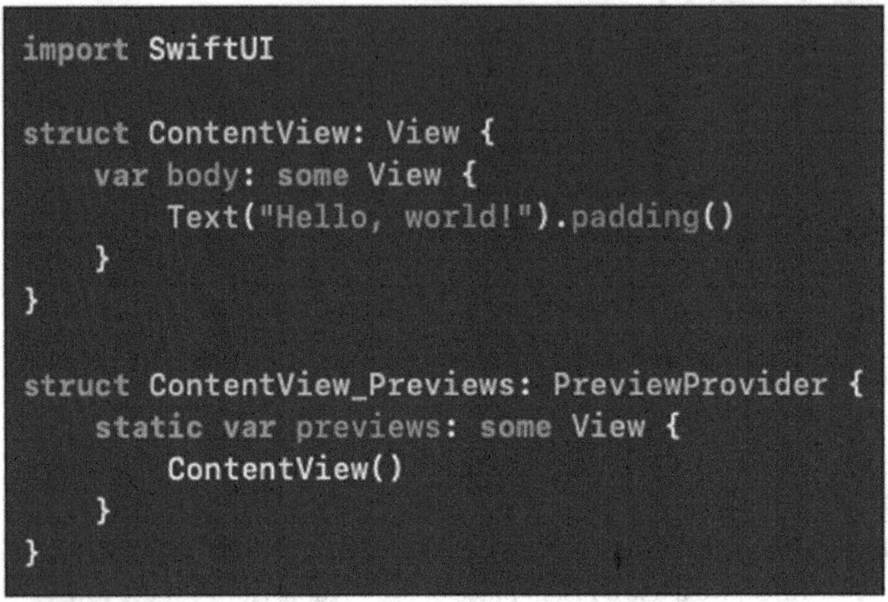

```
import SwiftUI

struct ContentView: View {
    var body: some View {
        Text("Hello, world!").padding()
    }
}

struct ContentView_Previews: PreviewProvider {
    static var previews: some View {
        ContentView()
    }
}
```

Figure 7-1. *Default New Project Code*

Let's create a simple list of some number of items. First, we'll delete the "Hello, World!" Text item. In its place, we'll add our list like this:

```
var body: some View {
    List(0..<19) { index in
        Text("\(index)")
    }
}
```

This creates a list of 20 items. Each item created is a Text UI element with the index number (Int) for the loop. The top of the preview canvas looks like Figure 7-2.

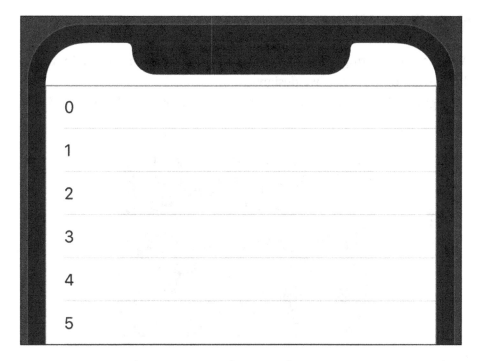

Figure 7-2. *List of Text Items with a Number*

The concept is very similar to what we've already seen. Instead of an HStack or VStack, our body property returns a List. We pass into the List a range of 0..<19, and for each pass it creates a Text element.

The closure we pass into the List call takes a parameter which I named index. It's an Int and it is the number in the range of the current iteration.

Easy. No cells, index path, or dequeuing prototype cells defined in Interface Builder.

But what if we want something more complex? Instead of a Text element, we can create whatever we want. We've been dealing with our Note objects so let's make a list of them.

NoteRow View

We'll start by creating a new file for our separate view. This will help with the preview of the row as we design it.

Right-click your main folder of your project and select "New File..." as in Figure 7-3.

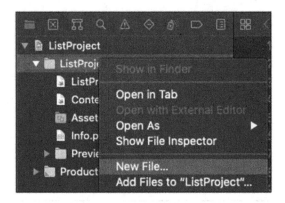

Figure 7-3. *New File...*

In the pop-up, filter for view and select SwiftUI View as in Figure 7-4. Click Next, name it NoteRow, and click Create.

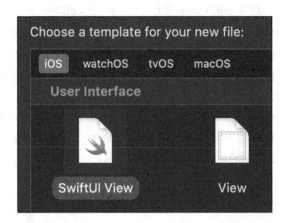

Figure 7-4. *SwiftUI View*

Initially, the NoteRow body property will be another Text with "Hello, World!". We'll replace that with something more along the lines of a row in a list.

Of course, our NoteRow needs a Note which hasn't been defined in this project (assuming you used a new project like I did). I'll define a Note class based on what we've done in previous chapters. It will look familiar as in Figure 7-5.

```swift
enum Priority : Int {
    case low, medium, high
}

class Note  {
    var text = "New Note" {
        didSet {
            self.updatedAtTime = Date()
        }
    }
    var updatedAtTime = Date()
    var priority = Priority.low {
        didSet {
            self.updatedAtTime = Date()
        }
    }
}
```

Figure 7-5. *Note Defined in NoteRow.swift*

It's a slightly simplified and cleaned version of what we've been using. It's good for what we'll be doing here.

If the NoteRow view has a Note instance, it can create a view that will look good in a list of notes. In our previous projects, the NoteView was not a great layout for a list. It was more square and chunky. We'd rather have something wider than tall and laid out in such a way that looks good when scrolling through the items.

We may not even choose to include all of the information about a Note. Depending on the app, having the updatedAtTime may not be useful to the user. For our example here, we'll put all of the information on the UI, but that's not always the case.

CREATING A LIST OF NOTES

We need to create NoteRow to display desired data about the Note. Once we have what we like, we can change out the List creation with NoteRows.

1. Add properties and an initializer to the NoteRow like this:

```
var note : Note
let df = DateFormatter()

init() {
    df.dateStyle = .none
    df.timeStyle = .medium
}
```

As in the past, this will force the creation of the NoteRow to require a Note to be passed in. Good.

2. Delete the Text item from the NoteRow body property.

You'll get some errors at this point, but we'll get rid of them quickly.

3. Within the body property, create a VStack with a Text item for the note's textfield:

```
var body: some View {
    VStack {
        Text(note.text)
    }
}
```

At this point, our body property is valid, but our preview doesn't work. That's because the creation of NoteRow in the NoteRow_Previews doesn't pass in a Note.

4. Update the NoteRow_Previews to pass in a note:

```
NoteRow(note: Note())
```

If you resume your preview, you should see "New Note" instead of "Hello, World!".

This is technically enough for a List, but let's flesh it out a bit more before jumping to that. But always feel free to experiment!

5. Under the text item in NoteRow's body, add an HStack with the priority star images like we had before:

```
HStack {
    Image(systemName: "star.circle")
    Image(systemName: note.priority.rawValue > 0 ?
        "star.circle" : "circle")
    Image(systemName: note.priority.rawValue > 1 ?
        "star.circle" : "circle")
}
```

6. Below the images you added in step 5, add another Text item for the Date value:

```
Text(df.string(from: note.updatedAtTime))
```

Now we're ready to create our List!

7. Back in ContentView, remove the Text item from the List in the body and replace it with creations of the NoteRow:

```
var body: some View {
    List(0..<19) { index in
        NoteRow(note: Note(), df: self.df)
    }
}
```

If you run the app or update the preview, it should look like
Figure 7-6.

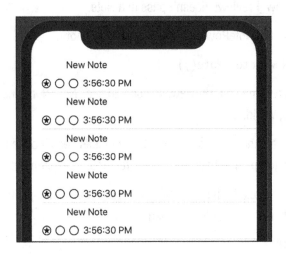

Figure 7-6. *List of Notes*

We did it! We have a List of Note items. The code is clear about what's
being done, and the List code is basically just one line of code.

But it can certainly look better. The note text should ideally be left
justified. And some space between the priority and the update time
would look good.

Let's head back to the NoteRow and make some changes based on
these ideas.

8. Back in NoteRow's VStack, let's add an alignment parameter:

```
VStack(alignment: .leading) {
```

9. Add a Spacer between the last star image and the Text item for
    the date:

```
Spacer()
```

10. Run the app or go back to the ContentView and refresh the preview. It should look like Figure 7-7.

Figure 7-7. *List of Notes with Updated NoteRow*

That's more like it. A real list! It's not too amazing, but it's pretty cool and quite easy to make. We basically took many of the things we already knew how to do and did them in a loop with a call to a List.

Model Listing

It's not very often you need to list a loop of numbers. Of course, what is common is listing an Array of items. Instead of passing in a range of numbers to a List, we can pass in a collection of Note instances.

A List has a variety of initializers with various parameters. Let's change our app to use an Array of Notes. For that, we'll need to add an array of Notes as a property.

105

Let's create a createTestNotes function on our Note object. We'll make it static so it can be called on the class:

```
static func createTestNotes() -> [Note] {
    var items = [Note]()
    for i in 0..<19 {
        let note = Note()
        note.text = "\(i)"
        items.append(note)
    }
    return items
}
```

By keeping the generation of this array outside of the ContentView, we avoid any mutating issues of the ContentView struct.

Now we can add a property to our ContentView to hold the Notes. We want this to have an @State property wrapper so updates get reflected in the List.

```
struct ContentView: View {
    let df = DateFormatter()
    @State private var notes = Note.createTestNotes()
```

Now we can update our List to use our notes array. The first parameter for the List will be our array: the notes property. The second parameter is a closure. The closure is called once for each item, and that Note is passed into the closure. We just need to create the NoteRow, and we already know how to do that:

```
List(notes) { note in
    NoteRow(note: note, df: self.df)
}
```

This produced an error because the Note items need to be identifiable. The List requires that the items are random access. All we need to do is have the Note conform to the Identifiable protocol.

That protocol requires an id property. We'll add one and initialize it to a UUID.

```
class Note : Identifiable { var id = UUID()
```

Now we get a clean build. Our code looks a little different from the last time we ran it, but the UI is the same (except for the note text value).

Once again, reality gets in the way. Typically, when you see a list of data you created, like notes, you expect to be able to delete from the list. The list doesn't have a modifier to handle this, but ForEach does. Let's see how that looks.

DELETE ITEMS IN LIST

We're still going to use a List, but we won't have it iterate our items. Previously, we used List to create a NoteRow for each of our array items. We'll still use List to display all the rows we create, but we'll create them in a different iteration.

1. Change the call of the List to ForEach:

```
ForEach(notes) { note in
    NoteRow(note: note, df: self.df)

}
```

This should compile and run still, but it won't look very good. :)

2. Wrap the ForEach call in a new List call:

```
List {
    ForEach(notes) { note in
        NoteRow(note: note, df: self.df)
    }
}
```

The app and preview should look better now. On to the deletion!

As I mentioned, the List doesn't have a modifier for deleting an item, but ForEach does. We can add the modifier which gets passed in the offset of the items to delete. And it just so happens that our array has a remove function that takes just that.

3. Add the onDelete modifier to the ForEach:

```
ForEach(notes, id: \.id) { note in
    NoteRow(note: note, df: self.df)
}
.onDelete { offsets in
    self.notes.remove(atOffsets: offsets)
}
```

With the ForEach handling the delete, the system provides the left swipe action with the "Delete" option like Figure 7-8.

Figure 7-8. *Delete Action on the List Row*

Tapping Delete causes the call on the closure passed into the onDelete definition. That will remove the row from the notes array. Since our notes array has an @State property wrapper, the List is redisplayed.

Notice that the animation is automatically performed, and it all works and looks great!

Chapter Summary

In this chapter, we learned about the List view struct. With a property-defined model, adding a List is very easy. At its core, the code is just looping over the array and creating a view for each item.

Our Note object is very similar to as it has been in previous chapters. However, we did make it conform to Identifiable by adding an id property. Also, we added a static method to create an array of test Note instances.

We created a NoteRow view to be displayed in the List. This could be really anything that implements a View. Ideally, this is going to be a view that looks good in a list.

By changing our List implementation to use a ForEach, we were able to easily add the deletion handling. Once our notes array had an @State property wrapper, deleting an item kept the UI in sync with the model.

A List has a lot of powerful uses and is used, like a table view, in most apps. It's a good idea to learn more of the modifiers and options for a List to use it to its full capacity.

CHAPTER 8

SwiftUI Canvas Preview

Designing a great UI may not be your task. Developing the UI design in SwiftUI code likely is since you're reading this book. If you've done it in the past with Interface Builder or even in code, you likely used Preview for your Storyboard. It shows you how the UI will look on a variety of devices.

However, you more likely ran the app in the simulator or on a device to have both real data and interaction. Of course, that takes more time: compiling, installing, running, and navigating. Then make a change to the UI or code and repeat.

The Canvas Preview allows you to see the UI right alongside your code. Not only that, but it actually compiles your code and shows you just how it will look at runtime. This includes data and functionality used in determining your user interface. This process is called "dynamic replacement."

The Preview is shown in the Canvas. I will continue to use those two terms together and interchangeably.

Let's look at the details of the Canvas/Preview.

Compiling

As I mentioned earlier, Xcode compiles your actual code to create and display the preview in the Canvas. Xcode knows what file you're working

© Bear Cahill 2021
B. Cahill, *UI Design for iOS App Development*,
https://doi.org/10.1007/978-1-4842-6449-2_8

on and what changes need to be compiled. It only compiles what's necessary to make the process as quick as possible.

In some cases, like changing a literal value, it doesn't even need to compile, and changes are done quite fast and automatically.

For more significant changes, like adding a property to a related object, the automatic updates are paused. In those cases, you'll see a message at the top left of the Canvas like Figure 8-1.

Figure 8-1. Preview Updating Paused

To continue updating the preview, click the Resume button in the pop-up message or on the top right of the Canvas.

The great thing about this preview is that it is *actually* the UI. This is your compiled SwiftUI code generating this preview. This means this is what your UI will look like at runtime using all of the data and functionality related to its presentation.

Changes are reflected in the preview as you make them. No more having to build, run, click/tap, and so on.

Preview Provider

In the previous chapter, we were working with a List of Note items. When we created the project with our default ContentView struct, we were also given a ContentView_Previews struct below it:

```
struct ContentView_Previews: PreviewProvider {
    static var previews: some View {
        ContentView()
    }
}
```

The same is true for our NoteRow. These are what Xcode uses to direct the specific compiling and rendering of our preview.

PreviewProvider is a protocol with a required computed property called previews. It's very similar to the required computed property defined by the View protocol we've been using.

Our previews property needs to return something that implements the View protocol just like the body property. So one easy way to do that, as the default implementation does, is to return an instance of our struct (e.g., ContentView).

If the initializer takes parameters, as our NoteRow does, we can pass those in as well:

```
struct NoteRow_Previews: PreviewProvider {
    static var previews: some View {
        NoteRow(note: Note(), df: DateFormatter())
    }
}
```

Preview Device

One way to change the preview in the Canvas is by changing the run destination. You can select various simulators from the drop-down to the right of the active scheme (top left in Xcode) for what device to use in the preview (see Figure 8-2).

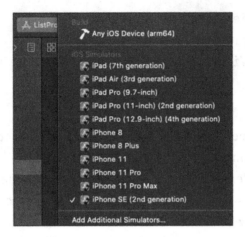

Figure 8-2. *Run Destination Selection*

Selecting a different simulator here will update the preview to use that device in the Canvas.

This is a quick and easy way to check the UI on various device sizes.

However, the Preview API allows for you to do this in the code as well with the .previewDevice modifier.

I have iPhone 11 Pro Max selected, but I want to see how it looks on the iPhone 8. I simply add the .previewDevice modifier to the ContentView() in my previews code:

```
struct ContentView_Previews: PreviewProvider {
    static var previews: some View {
        ContentView()
            .previewDevice("iPhone 8")
    }
}
```

My preview now displays the iPhone 8 in the Canvas like Figure 8-3.

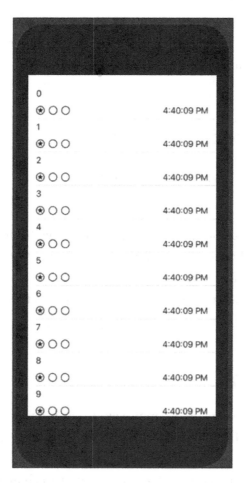

Figure 8-3. *iPhone 8 Preview*

Similarly, you can wrap multiple ContentView instances in a Group and display multiple device types in the Canvas.

This allows you to see how your UI will look on various devices, in real time at the same time.

A shortcut for embedding an item(s) into a Group is with the ⌘ + click and select the Group option.

Now your preview can return a group of ContentViews each with a different preview device.

If I want to preview an iPhone 8 and iPhone 11 at the same time, I can use each one of those in the .previewDevice modifier for my two ContentView instances like this in the code:

```
Group {
    ContentView()
        .previewDevice("iPhone 8")
    ContentView()
        .previewDevice("iPhone 11")
}
```

Now I see both devices in the Canvas and can view my updates as I change the SwiftUI code. This is particularly helpful when you're working on parts of your UI that take up the entire screen.

Sometimes, however, seeing the entire device isn't really what helps the most.

Environment

Along with multiple devices, we may want to see how various environment settings affect the UI. Seeing multiple options for things like dark mode at the same time can be very convenient.

Just like we chained the .previewDevice, we can chain a call to .environment. I'll add dark mode to one of my devices in the code:

```
ContentView()
    .previewDevice("iPhone 8")
    .environment(\.colorScheme, .dark)
ContentView()
    .previewDevice("iPhone 11")
```

Now my iPhone 8 preview will be in dark mode.

You may also want to see what your UI will look like with different text size selections; you can simulate other text size like this:

```
.environment(\.sizeCategory, .extraExtraExtraLarge)
```

Using a variety of ContentView previews with various settings can allow you to see at design time exactly how your UI will look when your app is executed.

If you have a collection of values, such as colorScheme and ContentSizeCategory, you may want to view them all. As we saw with List, we can use ForEach. Just like so many other things we've used, ForEach actually returns a View.

Each iteration of ForEach needs to return a View that is then used in the UI. Previously, we used it in a List. Each iteration returned a NoteRow. Now we can use it in the preview.

```
ForEach(ContentSizeCategory.allCases,
        id: \.self) { sizeCat in
            ContentView()
                .environment(\.colorScheme, .dark)
                .environment(\.sizeCategory, sizeCat)
}
```

As with the ForEach in the List previously, we have to provide a way for each item to be identified. This is particularly key in this case because Xcode needs to know which preview to update as necessary. We'll use the .self as the identity.

When using the List, we included each return of the ForEach (a NoteRow) in the list. In the preceding code, we're creating a full preview for each value in the ContentSizeCategory. That means we'll have a preview in the Canvas for each size the system text can be set to (over ten previews).

This is a lot of previews of the full UI for the text change that's really on the NoteRow View. Therefore, it would probably be better to add this type of variation to the NoteView preview instead of the ContentView.

Preview Layout

When you're working on a View that is only part of the screen, that's all you want to see. In our case, the NoteRow doesn't need the entire device screen in the Canvas. And having multiple of them doesn't help either.

In those cases, the .previewLayout modifier may work better. Not only do you not want multiple versions of the device, you may not want a device at all.

Our NoteRow is a good example of this. We don't really need to see the entire device (or multiple devices) to see what a NoteRow will look like.

I've changed the NoteRow_Previews code to include a static computed property for a DateFormatter.

```
static var dateFormatter : DateFormatter {
    let df = DateFormatter()
    df.dateStyle = .none
    df.timeStyle = .medium
    return df
}
```

Now my preview can pass in this new property when creating a NoteRow. My previews in NoteRow_Previews just returns

```
NoteRow(note: Note(),
        df: dateFormatter)
```

And the UI looks like Figure 8-4. This is a bit much for just a row for a list. Let's use .previewLayout to make it more reasonable and accurate to what we've designed.

Figure 8-4. *NoteRow in Preview*

After our NoteRow creation in the previews property, we'll call
.previewLayout with one of its three parameter options as we see in
Figure 8-5.

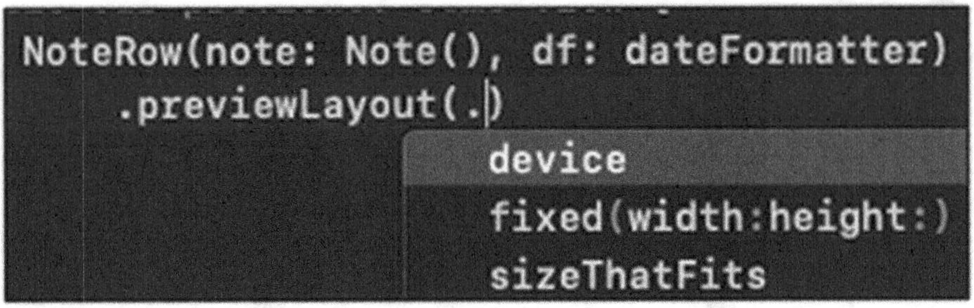

```
NoteRow(note: Note(), df: dateFormatter)
    .previewLayout(.|)
                        device
                        fixed(width:height:)
                        sizeThatFits
```

Figure 8-5. *Preview Layout Auto-complete Options*

As you can see with the device option selected, the description says it will be centered in the device in the preview. That's basically what we've been seeing all along. If you drill into .previewDevice, you can see a list of the supported devices such as

```
/// "iPhone 7"
/// "iPhone 7 Plus"
/// "iPhone 8"
/// "iPhone 8 Plus"
/// "iPhone SE"
/// "iPhone X"
/// "iPhone Xs"
/// "iPhone Xs Max"
/// "iPhone Xʀ"
/// "iPad mini 4"
/// "iPad Air 2"
/// "iPad Pro (9.7-inch)"
```

The fixed option takes a width and height. This is great for specifying a concrete width and height for your item. If you know the element you're designing will be a fixed size, this is how you can preview it just as it will be.

If I put in a width of 200 and height of 80, my NoteRow will look like Figure 8-6.

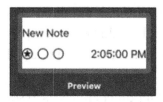

Figure 8-6. *NoteRow with Fixed Width and Height*

```
NoteRow(note: Note(), df: dateFormatter)
    .previewLayout(.fixed(width: 200, height: 80))
```

In reality, I'd probably want it to be wider, but you get the idea. I could give it a larger width and continue designing. I'd want to pick something that goes along with the look that helps me see it as a List element.

One issue specifically with this size is that the Spacer doesn't have much effect. I can't tell that it will expand and have more of an impact on the design.

Another option is the sizeThatFits value for PreviewLayout. This option, of course, causes the preview to use the size necessary for the View being created.

```
NoteRow(note: Note(), df: dateFormatter)
    .previewLayout(.sizeThatFits)
```

If I use this option, the UI preview looks like Figure 8-7.

Figure 8-7. *Preview Layout with sizeThatFits*

You may be wondering how it determined the width. We have a Spacer so in theory the width could be any size. It's using the simulator we picked. If we pick an iPad for the run destination, the NoteRow would be considerably wider.

And the .environment modifier allows us to specify other variations of the environment settings that might be in place for the user.

Let's put a lot of these to work together in our NoteRow View.

TEXT SIZES IN NOTEROW

In this exercise, we're going to add a ForEach to the NoteRow to see its preview with each of the content size category values.

1. Add a ForEach to the NoteRow_Previews:

```
ForEach(ContentSizeCategory.allCases,
        id: \.self) {
}
```

2. Set the closure parameter to be sizeCat:

```
ForEach(ContentSizeCategory.allCases,
        id: \.self) { sizeCat in
}
```

3. Inside the closure, create the NoteRow:

```
ForEach(ContentSizeCategory.allCases,
        id: \.self) { sizeCat in
            NoteRow(note: Note(), df: dateFormatter)
}
```

4. Add the .previewLayout with .sizeThatFits for the NoteRow:

```
NoteRow(note: Note(), df: dateFormatter)
    .previewLayout(.sizeThatFits)
```

122

5. Add the environment setting for the .sizeCategory key path
    using the sizeCat parameter:

```
NoteRow(note: Note(), df: dateFormatter)
    .previewLayout(.sizeThatFits)
    .environment(\.sizeCategory, sizeCat)
```

Update the preview to make sure several NoteRows are
displayed – one for each size category.

Let's take it one step further and distinguish each item in the
Canvas with a display name.

6. Chain a call to .previewDisplayName and pass in the
    sizeCat again.

```
.previewDisplayName("\(sizeCat)")
```

A partial version of the display is in Figure 8-8.

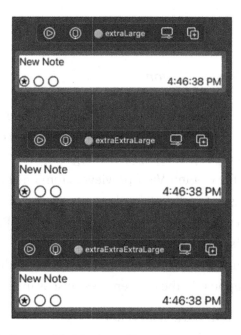

Figure 8-8. *NoteRow with Various Text Sizes*

We've isolated one UI element that can be used across our app. By using modifiers in the preview element, we can see a variety of ways it could be displayed.

Pin Preview

From all of these options, we may want to make some changes. If possible, you want to make your UI look great in all cases. That may require changes to the NoteRow or the ContentView.

Often, it's helpful to see the NoteRow changes while viewing the ContentView preview in the Canvas. This can be done by pinning the preview.

To pin the preview, have the preview up you want to remain in the Canvas. Then click the "Pin Preview" button on the bottom left of the Canvas as in Figure 8-9.

Figure 8-9. *Pin Preview Button*

When a preview is pinned, the icon will be blue (or whatever color you have set for your macOS system highlight color). You can unpin the preview, even from other previews, by clicking it again.

This will cause the ContentView preview to remain at the top of the Canvas as you navigate to other View elements. As you make changes to your NoteRow, you will see how it looks both as the NoteRow and within the ContentView List.

If I change my updatedAtTime text to have a font modifier for .thin, I can see it as it will appear in the ContentView List as in Figure 8-10.

```
Text(df.string(from: note.updatedAtTime))
    .fontWeight(.thin)
```

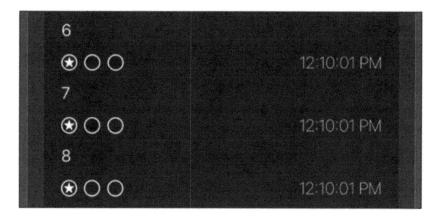

Figure 8-10. *NoteRow Updated in the ContentView Preview*

Chapter Summary

In this chapter, we've seen how a preview item is created for our various View items. Using modifiers can allow us to see how the UI will display in different devices, environments, and layouts.

We also used ForEach to show a variety of previews for our item in the Canvas. This can greatly speed up development by avoiding time in builds, installs, execution, and navigation to check the user interface. With a small amount of code, you can see your UI with different color schemes, text sizes, locales, and more.

By passing in data, a Note instance, to our NoteRow, we provided the data to the row. However, it was the same data each time. Next, we'll look at using Preview Content and other tools to use more realistic data.

CHAPTER 9

Design for Previews

The Canvas is a powerful tool when designing the UI of your app. However, it's more than that. Since the previews shown in the Canvas are the actual user interface, it shouldn't be considered just a "preview" in the typical sense. Similarly, since it runs related code, it shouldn't be considered just the UI.

Previews in the Canvas are closer to the simulator than the past. With Interface Builder, the UI was just the design of the interface. And the Preview of the past was a fairly lifeless rendering of that interface.

Just as the user interface design has been changed into code in SwiftUI, the Canvas brings the simulator into the development. This not only changes how you develop the visual elements of your app. It should change how you approach the organization of your code.

We need to consider the previews in developing our code to take full advantage of the power of previews.

Preview Content

So far in our app, we've been using default data. Our preview reflects this limitation. Wouldn't it be better to use more realistic data? But we may not have access to a database or server API yet. Even if we did, would we want to use those for every rendering of the UI in the Canvas? Probably not.

SwiftUI provides a group in new projects called "Preview Content" (see Figure 9-1).

© Bear Cahill 2021
B. Cahill, *UI Design for iOS App Development*,
https://doi.org/10.1007/978-1-4842-6449-2_9

Note   This group is not there for multiplatform projects.

Figure 9-1. *Preview Content Group in a Project*

The Preview Content group has an assets catalog already created in it. You can put images to use in previews in this catalog. You can put other preview-related files in the Preview Content to be used for previews as well.

By default, this group is not included in Debug and Release builds per the Build Settings (see Figure 9-2).

▼ Development Assets	"ListProject/Preview Content"
Debug	"ListProject/Preview Content"
Release	"ListProject/Preview Content"

Figure 9-2. *Build Settings for Development Assets*

Notice that it's the "Preview Content" group that is listed to be excluded. So anything you add under that group (e.g., files, other groups, more assets catalogs) won't be included in your builds for testers or release.

Preview JSON

A great way to simulate data (especially from an API) is with a JSON file. We can add a JSON file to our Preview Content for our previews. Then we know we have readily available data to build our previews with, and it will be automatically excluded from our builds.

Here's some JSON data that we can use for our notes:

```
[
    {
        "id": "FAF80C6A-F1C3-44D9-9539-D6113777520C",
        "text": "I'm note 0", "updatedAtTime": 1000,
        "priority": 2,
        "image": "note1",
        "dueDate": 1598923198
    },
    {
        "id": "FAF80C6A-F1C3-44D9-9539-D6113777520B",
        "text": "I'm note 1",
        "updatedAtTime": 2000,
        "priority": 1,
        "image": "note2",
        "dueDate": 620606310
    }
]
```

You may notice that there's some fields in there that we don't have in our current Note class. The additional fields are image and dueDate.

These items weren't used in our UI so we didn't need them, but now we're going to add them. So we can create this as a text file and add it to our project or create it with the "New File…" menu option from right-clicking Preview Content (in this case, select an Empty File). I've named mine Data.json.

Model

We need to change our model just a bit to reflect these additions. We need to add an image property of type String and dueDate as a Date.

We can initialize them as empty string ("") and a distant future date (Date.distantFuture).

While we're here, let's also delete the CreateTestNotes function as in Figure 9-3. We're going to load the test notes differently going forward.

```
class Note : Identifiable, Codable {
    var id = UUID().uuidString
    var text = "New Note" {
        didSet {
            self.updatedAtTime = Date()
        }
    }
    var updatedAtTime = Date()
    var priority = Priority.low {
        didSet {
            self.updatedAtTime = Date()
        }
    }
    var image = ""
    var dueDate = Date.distantFuture
    var isPastDue : Bool {
        dueDate < Date()
    }
}
```

Figure 9-3. Note Class as the Model

Since we're going to load the instances of Note objects based on the JSON file, we want them to conform to the Codable protocol. The property names and JSON field names match already so we just need to specify that in the declaration.

Our Priority enumeration also needs to be Codable by simply adding the protocol to the declaration:

```
enum Priority : Int, Codable
```

Of course, the isPastDue property is computed. It's not in the JSON and won't be parsed from the data file.

Our model now focuses on just the data. We're trying to separate out our model and view a bit more. This will allow us to isolate the model, the view, and the data to display: view model.

While we're in the enum, let's add an implementation for the CaseIterable protocol. The protocol gives us access to the enum values in an array property called allCases. We can use that to return the max value of the enum.

```
enum Priority : Int, Codable, CaseIterable {
    case low, medium, high

    static var max : Int {
        Priority.init(rawValue:
            Priority.allCases.count - 1)!
            .rawValue
    }
}
```

View Model

The view model is where we will have the data in the model mapped to the data to display. For example, our priority is an enumeration mapping to 0, 1, and 2 for low, medium, and high, respectively. But visually we want to display those as star and circle images. Our view model will do that mapping.

Our new NoteViewModel class will have properties related to the Note (model) class. These properties will effectively define the mapping of the model data to the view. For example, instead of a priority property, we have a priorityImages property. It's an array of strings representing the names of the images for the UI to display.

Also, since the view model is responsible for mapping the various values, this is now where we can store the DateFormatter. These properties are defined as in Figure 9-4.

```swift
class NoteViewModel : Identifiable {
    var id = UUID().uuidString
    var text = ""
    var priorityImages : [String]
    var time = ""
    var imageName = ""
    var renderingColor = Color(UIColor.label)

    static var dateFormatter : DateFormatter {
        let df = DateFormatter()
        df.dateStyle = .none
        df.timeStyle = .medium
        return df
    }
}
```

Figure 9-4. *NoteViewModel as the View Model Class*

We will be iterating over an array of NoteViewModel instances so it conforms to the Identifiable protocol and has an id property of a UUID string.

Notice the renderingColor. We will set this value based on the isPastDue value from the note. The default rendering color is UIColor. label. This is to make the rendering dark for light mode and vice versa.

Clearly, a Note instance will need to be passed into an initializer for NoteViewModel:

```
init(model : Note) {
    text = model.text
    time = NoteViewModel.dateFormatter.string(from:
            model.updatedAtTime)
    renderingColor = model.isPastDue ? Color.red :
            renderingColor
    imageName = model.image
    priorityImages = Array(repeating: "star.circle",
            count: model.priority.rawValue + 1)
    priorityImages += Array(repeating: "circle",
            count: Priority.max -
                model.priority.rawValue)
}
```

Our initializer stores the text from the model (Note) passed in. It then formats and sets the time property based on the updatedAtTime from the Note.

The renderingColor is based off of the isPastDue value. It's red if it's past the due date. Otherwise, it uses the existing, default color.

The image value is stored in the imageName property.

For the priorityImages, we want to repeat the star.circle image as many times as the raw value of the priority plus one. So for low priority (0), we want one star. Then we fill in the rest (max – priority raw value) with circles.

The last thing our view model needs is a way to load the JSON data. We could do this in other places in the code, but since our goal is to generate test NoteViewModel instances, I'd like to put it in the NoteViewModel class as in Figure 9-5.

```
#if DEBUG
static func loadTestData() -> [NoteViewModel] {
    guard let url = Bundle.main.url(forResource: "Data",
                                    withExtension: "json"),
        let data = try? Data(contentsOf: url),
        let notes = try? JSONDecoder().decode([Note].self,
                                              from: data)
        else { return [] }
    return notes.map { NoteViewModel(model: $0) }
}
#endif
```

Figure 9-5. *Loading Test Data into View Model Instances*

Similarly, all of these classes, structs, and enums could be organized in other files. You may want your model classes in their own group. View Model objects could be in a ViewModel group as well.

This method gets the URL to the file, loads it into a Data instance, parses it into Note instances, and maps those Notes into an array of NoteViewModel instances.

It's a static function so it can be called without having a NoteViewModel instance.

Also, note the "#if DEBUG" compilation condition. Swift doesn't have a preprocessor, but it does handle the same flags during compilation. In this case, we don't want this function included in our release builds.

Now we have our model (Note) loaded and converted into our view model (NoteViewModel). We need to update our View (NoteRow) to use the model view.

View

Our NoteRow will be simplified both in the data it needs and converting data to the UI. It no longer needs a DateFormatter object. It only needs a NoteViewModel:

```
struct NoteRow: View {
    var noteVM : NoteViewModel
```

The UI will still contain the same items: text, priority stars, spacer, and time it was updated. However, now the NoteRow can just get what it needs from the NoteViewModel and make decisions only regarding the layout.

Using its NoteViewModel property, it can get the text, display the three images in priorityImages, and set the time from the view model's time property.

The NoteRow will also use the renderingColor on the stars and time. The view model has already determined what the color is based on its own logic. The body property code looks like Figure 9-6.

```
var body: some View {
    VStack(alignment: .leading) {
        Text(noteVM.text)
        HStack {
            ForEach(noteVM.priorityImages, id: \.self)
            { (imageName) in
                Image(systemName: imageName)
                    .foregroundColor(self.noteVM.renderingColor)
            }
            Spacer()
            Text(noteVM.time)
                .fontWeight(.thin)
                .foregroundColor(self.noteVM.renderingColor)
        }
    }
}
```

Figure 9-6. NoteRow's body Property Using the NoteViewModel Property

Again, notice that NoteRow only makes decisions based on the layout of the UI: VStack, HStack, ForEach, Spacer, and so on.

All this work to separate out classes based on their roles of the Model, View, and View Model. It may not seem like we've gained much, but in regard to the preview, we have.

Preview

Our NoteRow_Previews can be a good bit simpler and agnostic to the Model and View Model. It basically just has to relate and return them.

Also, we can create a row in a ForEach loop for each item in our JSON data. How does that pay off? It means we can create variations in our test data that mimic what can happen in real data. When the data has a new variation (e.g., a new priority value), we can create test data to represent it and see how the UI reacts.

PREVIEW THE TEST DATA

In this exercise, we'll update our NoteRow_Previews struct to display our test JSON data. We need to load that data and create a NoteRow for each item in the file.

1. Clear out the previews computed property in the NoteRow_Previews:

```
static var previews: some View {
}
```

2. Add a ForEach using the NoteViewModel loadTestData call:

```
ForEach(NoteViewModel.loadTestData(), id: \.id)
{ (noteVM) in }
```

3. In the ForEach loop, create NoteRow instances with the View Model passed in:

```
{ (noteVM) in
    NoteRow(noteVM: noteVM)
}
```

4. Use previewLayout (and/or other modifiers) to display each row as desired:

```
NoteRow(noteVM: noteVM)
    .previewLayout(.sizeThatFits)
```

Note   You may need to comment out the bulk of your ContentView to make your project compile. For your body and previews computed properties, you can just return a Text item for now.

---

5. Verify the preview looks as you would expect it to in the Canvas as in Figure 9-7.

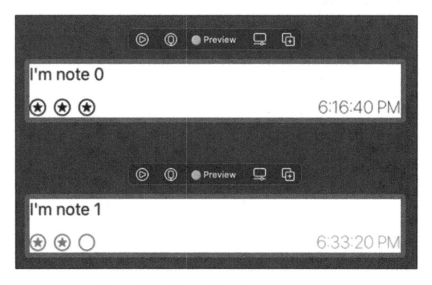

Figure 9-7. *Preview of NoteRow_Previews*

In my test data, I used dates such that my first note is not past due but my second note is.

Now we have our test data loading and rendered in the preview for our NoteRow. You can create more JSON items to view more variations of the rows in your Canvas.

Preview Assets

You may have realized we aren't using the image value from the JSON data. To do that, we need images. My test data contains two Note items with image values of note1 and note2. We want to display those in our rows too.

First, we need to have images with those names in our project. We'll add these to the "Preview Assets.xcassets" catalog in our Preview Content group. By doing this, the images won't be included in our builds for testing and release.

I dropped two images in my "Preview Assets.xcassets" named note1 and note2 as in Figure 9-8.

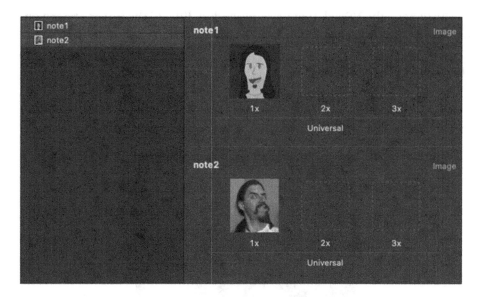

Figure 9-8. *Images Note1 and Note2 in "Preview Assets.xcassets"*

For my UI, I want the image to appear on the left side of the row. To do that, I'll embed my VStack in an HStack. I can ⌘ + click the VStack and select "Embed in HStack" as in Figure 9-9.

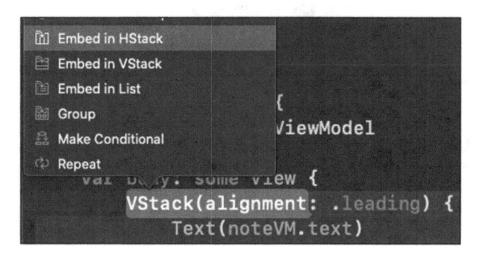

Figure 9-9. *Embed VStack in an HStack*

Just above the VStack that was embedded, I'll add the images based on the NoteViewModel imageName property.

```
Image(noteVM.imageName)
```

Because my two images aren't the same size, the preview looks a bit off in the Canvas as in Figure 9-10.

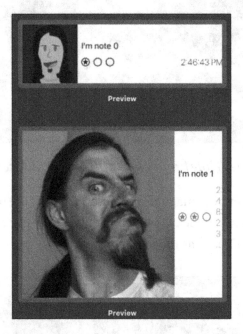

Figure 9-10. *Images in the NoteRow*

We can use a few modifiers on the Image to make it more uniform. First, we need to make the image resizable. This will make sure that when we change the frame of the image, the image will resize too. Optionally, we can pass in some insets and a resizing mode, but we'll take the defaults. Feel free to play around with those.

Resizable is a modifier on the Image element so we need to call that first.

```
Image(noteVM.imageName)
    .resizable()
    .frame(width: 100.0,height:100)
```

The returned Image from resizable also conforms to View so we can use the .frame modifier on that. Setting the width and height to something reasonable will make the row look good again like Figure 9-11.

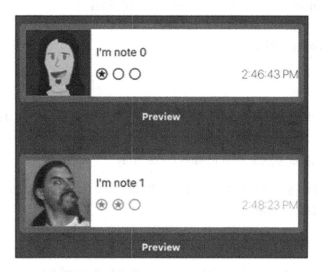

Figure 9-11. *NoteRow with Images Sized Equally*

Now we just need to use this in our ContentView!

```
USE NOTEROW IN CONTENTVIEW
```

We'll be pretty much starting over with our ContentView. The starting code can look like this:

```
struct ContentView: View {
    var body: some View {
    }
}

struct ContentView_Previews: PreviewProvider {
    static var previews: some View {
        ContentView()
    }
}
```

Our code will be fairly simple. The ContentView needs the data to be displayed. We'll use an array of NoteViewModel instances. The body will create a List of NoteRows based on the view models in the array.

1. Create a property in ContentView to store the NoteViewModel instances in an array.

   ```
   @State private var items = [NoteViewModel]()
   ```

2. In the body, create a List item and within that a ForEach loop over the array property from step 1.

   ```
   List {
       ForEach(items, id: \.id)
          { }
   ```

3. In the closure of the ForEach, create instances of NoteRow using the NoteViewModel passed in from the loop (I'm using shorthand argument names, i.e., $0).

```
ForEach(items, id: \.id)
    { NoteRow(noteVM: $0) }
```

Update your preview. Notice there are no rows. Why? We didn't load the test data. We could initialize the data in our ContentView_Previews, but the property is private.

4. Add an .onDelete modifier to your ForEach.

```
ForEach(items, id: \.id)
    { NoteRow(noteVM: $0) }
    .onDelete { offsets in
        self.items.remove(atOffsets: offsets)
}
```

5. Initialize the NoteViewModel instances with a compilation condition.

```
#if DEBUG
@State private var items =
    NoteViewModel.loadTestData()

#else
@State private var items = [NoteViewModel]()

#endif
```

Now when we execute the app in debug, it will load the test data. Builds for testing and release won't include this in the compilation so there's no danger there.

Later when you want to test against live data, you can remove this code or modify it accordingly.

6. Refresh the preview and view the cells created as in Figure 9-12.

Figure 9-12. *ContentView Preview with NoteRows*

This is starting to look like a real app! It's based on test data, but who's to say our data wouldn't be stored in a JSON file within the app? Seeing it in the ContentView, we now have our Model, View, and View Model working end to end.

Live Mode

If we want to see it in action, we can click the Live Preview button. This button is on the right side of the icon bar above the preview. It appears as a play button as in Figure 9-13.

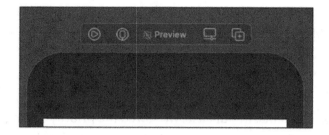

Figure 9-13. *Live Preview Button in the Icon Bar*

The preview doesn't change too much. The Live Preview button changes from a "play" icon to a "stop" icon. But the preview itself is live. We can interact with it as we would in the simulator or a physical device.

We can delete items by swiping as in Figure 9-14.

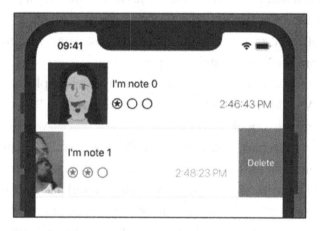

Figure 9-14. *Live Preview Interaction*

Chapter Summary

In this chapter, we added content, images, and data to our "Preview Content" group in the project. We used this data in our previews, but it won't be included in our builds. It's just for the Preview as it is named.

We refactored our code to split out the data to be stored from the JSON file into our Model class named Note. This class has little to do with any functionality and nothing to do with the UI directly.

Our new NoteViewModel class houses the version of the data to be displayed by the UI. This class does some massaging of the properties for proper visual elements. In our case, we stored the priority setting in the Note to a series of strings for our star/circle images. It also determines the rendering color based on the isPastDue from the Note.

Our NoteViewModel is created with a Note instance to have all the data it needs. Its loadTestData function loads the JSON file data and creates the notes and NoteViewModels for our previews.

We similarly refactored our NoteRow to focus on the UI aspects. The only decisions it makes are in regard to the UI. The data is all provided by the View Model.

The NoteRow_Previews now just loads the test data and creates NoteRows from the View Model instances.

The ContentView benefits from all of this by now simply having an array of NoteViewModels which loops over to create NoteRows in a List.

By isolating the model, view model, and view pieces, we can more easily focus on each part separately. This allows us to edit and preview pieces separated out as they will appear in their respective previews. And as we're seeing, the preview (especially in Live mode) basically is the app.

This leads to a bit of a mindset shift. We don't need to see developing our app as UI, functionality, and execution. We can basically do all three at once.

By focusing on designing our code for the preview, we are working on the entire app in a streamlined and seamless fashion.

CHAPTER 10

SwiftUI Navigation

We don't want to just list items usually. We want to allow the user to tap on those items and display details or edit items. Using our Notes app, we want to display details when a list item is tapped.

You are, no doubt, familiar with the typical conventions of navigation in an app. We'll look at the two most common. First, we'll see how to tap a row item and display a view modally sliding up from the bottom.

Second, we'll look at adding a navigation view to the app. This will allow the navigation to slide views in from the right. This is the standard "drill down" navigation for viewing details of a selection.

In both cases, we need to know which row the user tapped.

On Tap Gesture

To allow a view to slide up, we need to know when a user taps on a given item. Then, based on the items selected, we need to display related information.

This breaks down into three steps: tap, identify data tapped, and display the data.

For the tap, we can add the .onTapGesture modifier when we create each row. The same context is in scope. So in the code for the tap gesture, we have access to the same data used to create the row.

© Bear Cahill 2021
B. Cahill, *UI Design for iOS App Development*,
https://doi.org/10.1007/978-1-4842-6449-2_10

In our ListProject ContentView, we have our List. Adding a tap gesture to a NoteRow looks like this:

```
ForEach(items, id: \.id) { (noteVM)  in
    NoteRow(noteVM: noteVM)
    .onTapGesture {
        self.selectedNoteVM = noteVM
    }
}
```

Notice we are now accessing the note view model item in the tap gesture code. So the shorthand argument name ($0) no longer works for both scopes, and I added the noteVM parameter name.

The preceding code also stores the noteVM in a property of our ContentView. This is where we are now saving the data based on the user's selection. In our code, we can add the property like this:

```
var selectedNoteVM : NoteViewModel?
```

You'll notice you get a compile error now. The error states that "self" is immutable. That's true. So what do we do?

Fortunately, we ultimately want our UI to be updated based on this tap. That means we want our UI invalidated and rendered again based on this tap. Boiled down, we want the state to change so the interface is updated.

As we've seen before, what we really want to use here is a binding wrapper of our property as opposed to the property itself. First, we need to specify that our property is the source of truth for the selected item.

```
@State var selectedNoteVM : NoteViewModel?
```

So far, the code changes overall are pretty basic. We added a new property and added the tap gesture to the NoteRow creation like in Figure 10-1.

```
@State var selectedNoteVM : NoteViewModel?

var body: some View {
    List {
        ForEach(items, id: \.id) { (noteVM)  in
            NoteRow(noteVM: noteVM)
                .onTapGesture {
                    self.selectedNoteVM = noteVM
                }
        }
        .onDelete { offsets in
            self.items.remove(atOffsets: offsets)
        }
    }
}
```

Figure 10-1. *On Tap Gesture for List Items*

Now that we have the user's selected data, we need to display a new view.

Modal Navigation

For displaying a view modally, we'll use the .sheet modifier. This will be a modifier on the View item we return. In the case of our ListProject, that's the List item. So the .sheet modifier goes after the closing curly brace of our List item in the body property.

If you start to type .sheet after the List's closing curly brace, you'll see the auto-complete options as in Figure 10-2.

```
.sheet
M  sheet(item:content:)
M  sheet(isPresented:content:)
M  sheet(item:onDismiss:content:)
M  sheet(isPresented:onDismiss:content:)
```

Figure 10-2. *Sheet Modifier Auto-complete Options*

The first parameter is a Binding for either an Identifiable (item) or a Bool (isPresented). Both require a content closure that returns a View. If you choose the Identifiable, it will also be passed into the content closure.

They also both have an optional onDismiss closure. That closure is called when the sheet is dismissed.

If your @State property is a boolean, you can set it to true in cases for presenting the sheet. Then the content closure is called without a parameter. The view returned by the closure would need to be created without data or other properties already set.

In our case, we already have a source of truth binding for our selectedNoteVM; we can use that as our binding. Once it's set, the sheet closure is called with the binding. In our case, that's the note view model of the row. We can use that to create and return a view.

For example, we can create a Text item with the note view model's text.

```
.sheet(item: $selectedNoteVM) { (noteVM)
    in Text(noteVM.text)
}
```

When tapping on a row, selectedNoteVM is set in the tap gesture closure. That being set causes the .sheet closure to be called. The selectedNoteVM is passed in as the noteVM parameter. The new Text view is displayed as in Figure 10-3.

Figure 10-3. *Text Item Displayed After Row Tapped*

We added an .onTapGesture modifier to the NoteRow view in the List. In that closure, when called, we store the selected note view model item in a @State source of truth property.

When the property is set, the .sheet closure is called with the item. That closure returns the view, in our case a Text item, to display modally. To return to the previous view, swipe the view down to dismiss it.

You may want to display an "about page" or similar where you don't need data selected. In that case, the boolean binding might be a better choice.

Also, you might want to perform some action when the view is dismissed. In that case, you can provide the onDismiss closure as a parameter as well.

But what about navigating for sliding views in from the right? For that, we need a NavigationView.

Navigation View

Using a navigation view to display details isn't complex. However, it's very different from the modal route we saw earlier.

We won't use the .sheet modifier so we don't need the @State property wrapper. Since we don't need that, we don't need to set it either. That means we don't need the .onTapGesture modifier. So we can remove all of those: selectedNoteVM property and .sheet and .onTapGesture modifiers.

Our body property in ContentView is back to just the List and ForEach with the .onDelete modifier.

```
var body: some View {
    List {
        ForEach(items, id: \.id) { (noteVM) in
            NoteRow(noteVM: noteVM)
        }
        .onDelete { offsets in
            self.items.remove(atOffsets: offsets)
        }
    }
}
```

We want to wrap whatever we are navigating from in a NavigationView. Since it's a View, we can return that from our body property.

If we simply wrap our List in a NavigationView, our preview looks like Figure 10-4 in the Canvas.

Figure 10-4. *Navigation View Wrapping the List*

Notice that there is now a navigation bar at the top, but it's empty. The title is added as a modifier on the item contained in the NavigationView.

In the case of our ListProject, the List is the contained item. We use the .navigationTitle with a string (e.g., Notes) to set the title in the navigation bar.

```
NavigationView {
    List {
        ForEach(items, id: \.id) { (noteVM) in
            NoteRow(noteVM: noteVM)
        }
        .onDelete { offsets in
            self.items.remove(atOffsets: offsets)
        }
    }.navigationTitle("Notes")
}
```

Now our bar has a title as in Figure 10-5.

Figure 10-5. *Navigation Bar Title*

There are other modifiers for the navigation bar. In addition to the title, there are modifiers for setting the style, back button, left/right items, and more.

Now that we have our NavigationView, let's look at navigating.

Navigation Link

For modal navigation, we used the .onTapGesture modifier. In the related closure, we set a state property. That caused the .sheet modifier to be called and display a View returned from its closure.

For the NavigationView, we'll create NavigationLinks. A NavigationLink conforms to the View protocol. That means we can use it in our List. We'll return NavigationLink instances instead of NoteRows. And each NoteRow will be within the NavigationLink.

The NavigationLink initializers allow for various parameters. Particularly, they receive the destination and label. The destination is the View to display when the item is tapped. In our ListProject, we want some details of the selected note row to be displayed.

The label parameter is a closure. The closure returns a View to display as the item to be tapped. In our case, that's the row.

```
ADDING NAVIGATION TO LISTPROJECT
```

This exercise will go through the steps to add navigation to the ListProject app. The navigation to be added will slide in from the right for details.
We will use the NavigationView and NavigationLink in this exercise.

The first two steps are implementing the items discussed earlier. You may have already completed them if you were following along.

1. Wrap the existing List item in a NavigationView (unless you already did this by following along earlier).

```
NavigationView {
    List {
        ForEach(items, id: \.id) { (noteVM)    in
            NoteRow(noteVM: noteVM)
        }
        .onDelete { offsets in
            self.items.remove(atOffsets: offsets)
        }
    }
}
```

2. Add a Navigation Bar Title modifier to the List view (unless you already did this by following along earlier).

```
NavigationView {
    List {
        ForEach(items, id: \.id) { (noteVM)    in
            NoteRow(noteVM: noteVM)
        }
        .onDelete { offsets in
            self.items.remove(atOffsets: offsets)
        }
    }.navigationTitle("Notes")
}
```

3. Update the Preview and verify it looks similar to Figure 10-5.

4. Within the ForEach of the List, create a NavigationLink with a
    Text destination and NoteRow returned from the label closure.

    ```
    NavigationLink(destination: Text(noteVM.text)) {
        NoteRow(noteVM: noteVM)
    }
    ```

5. Run (simulator, device, or Live mode) the app and verify tapping
    on an item displays the details as in Figure 10-6.

Figure 10-6. *Navigation Within the App*

Notice that the navigation automatically includes the back button. And that the
back button is titled the same as the navigation bar title.

As you'd expect, tapping the back button returns to the previous view.

This exercise shows how quickly and easily you can add navigation from a List
(or other Views) to an app.

Chapter Summary

In this chapter, we looked at two common ways to navigate in an app. For modal navigation, we used the .sheet modifier. We added this modifier to the View our body parameter returned.

The .sheet modifier is given a binding to a property to determine when to display. We used a @State property wrapper for a note view model to set this condition.

To determine when a user tapped a row, we used the .onTapGesture modifier on each row. This provides the means to redisplay the UI and provide the necessary data to the .sheet closure.

For the hierarchy/drill-down style of navigation with a stack of views, we used the NavigationView. The contained view in the NavigationView uses the .navigationTitle modifier to set the title of the View.

The NavigationView provides the means of navigation. The NavigationLink provides the user interaction capabilities. A List item's ForEach creates the Views for the rows. NavigationLink also implements a View and can be used as the row items.

A NavigationLink needs to know what label (View) to display for the user tap. It also needs a destination (View) it will display when tapped. We used our NoteRow as the tappable area. When tapped, we provided a Text item of the note text to display.

We provided a simple View (i.e., Text) as the destination. Of course, more useful and interesting Views can be used instead.

CHAPTER 11

UIKit in SwiftUI

There will likely be times for various reasons you'll want to use UIKit in your SwiftUI app. No problem.

You may have an existing UI you need to use. Maybe you don't have time to update or just don't want to update it. Whether it's an existing View or your custom view, it can be done. Plus, any existing constraints are respected.

In this chapter, we'll look at incorporating existing UIKit classes into SwiftUI. This has been considered already for you. It's not a hack or even discouraged.

There's a bit of work to do, but the steps have already been laid out for you.

UIViewRepresentable

SwiftUI provides a protocol specifically for including UIView instances into your code. Basically, we're going to create a View struct that returns a UIView class.

The UIViewRepresentable protocol inherits from View. However, it specifies it to be a View that doesn't implement the body computed property. So it's a View but not like we've seen before.

Instead the protocol defines a function to be implemented. The makeUIView function UIKit classes into SwiftUI needs to return a UIView. Simple.

It's also passed in a Context for any values you might need to retrieve.

When the state changes and it's time to update the UI, there's another function: updateUIView. This function is called when there are

© Bear Cahill 2021
B. Cahill, *UI Design for iOS App Development*,
https://doi.org/10.1007/978-1-4842-6449-2_11

changes in any bindings. In the function code, you will update the UI programmatically based on the changes.

Optionally, you can implement the dismantleUIView. This is called when the memory is being cleaned up. If you need to do any last-minute actions as the UIView is being removed, this is your chance.

Instead of displaying the note's text when tapping on a row, we'll display the note details.

If you are working on macOS, the comparable protocol is NSViewRepresentable. Similarly, WatchKit views can be used with WKInterfaceObjectRepresentable.

NoteView

I've added a NoteView to the project. It's a basic View struct that displays some of the Note information; see Figure 11-1.

```swift
struct NoteView : View {
    @Binding var noteVM : NoteViewModel

    var body: some View {
        VStack {
            HStack {
                Spacer()
                Text("Updated At: \(noteVM.time)")
            }
            Spacer()
            Text(noteVM.text)
                .border(Color.gray, width: 1)
            Spacer()
            Image(noteVM.imageName)
                .resizable()
                .aspectRatio(contentMode: .fit)
        }.padding()
    }
}
```

Figure 11-1. NoteView Code

NoteView has a binding property for a NoteViewModel. This is used in the body to display the details. A VStack contains Text items for the updated at time and the note's text and an Image item for the related image.

The preview code loads the test data and displays an item. The code is in Figure 11-2.

```
struct NoteView_Previews: PreviewProvider {
    @State static var noteVM =
        NoteViewModel.loadTestData().last!
    static var previews: some View {
        NoteView(noteVM: $noteVM)
    }
}
```

Figure 11-2. *NoteView Preview Code*

The preview in the Canvas looks like Figure 11-3.

Figure 11-3. *NoteView*

Now let's use this when a row is tapped in our List.

161

DISPLAY DETAILS WITH NOTEVIEW

Currently, our ForEach in the ContentView uses a Text item to display the note text when a row is tapped. We want to change that to use NoteView.

However, if you just change the destination to NoteView, you'll get an error.

```
NavigationLink(destination:
    NoteView(noteVM: noteVM)) {
        NoteRow(noteVM: noteVM)
}
```

This is because the noteVM in the ForEach isn't bindable. It's just a locally scoped parameter. It needs to be the instance from the binding we have in the items array property.

1. Change the ForEach to iterate over the indices of the array.

   ```
   ForEach(items.indices) { (noteIndex) in
   ```

2. Change the destination parameter to be a NoteView.

   ```
   NavigationLink(destination:
   NoteView(noteVM: self.$items[noteIndex])) {
       NoteRow(noteVM: noteVM)
   }
   ```

3. Change the NoteRow creation to use the index.

   ```
   NavigationLink(destination:
   NoteView(noteVM: self.$items[noteIndex])) {
       NoteRow(noteVM: self.items[noteIndex])
   }
   ```

4. Run the apsp and verify the list looks the same and the details
    look like Figure 11-3.

By creating a fairly simple new view, we can display the details of a Note. We had
to change the ForEach to use the model data so that the binding would work.

Extracting a View

One thing missing from our note details is the priority. It would be nice to
have that, of course. But it would be better if we could reuse the code we
already wrote.

We can do that by extracting that part of NoteRow into its own View
struct. In NoteRow, we have an HStack that includes the priority star
images and the updated at time. If we command-click (⌘ + click) the
HStack, we see a menu as in Figure 11-4.

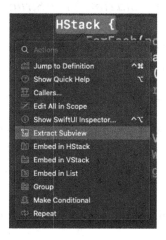

Figure 11-4. *Command-Click Menu*

We want to extract the view, and there's a menu item just for that. If we
click that item, it will extract the code and allow us to set a name for the
new View struct. I'll name mine NotePriorityAndTime.

163

However, we have a compile error since our new View doesn't have access to the noteVM value. No problem. We can add that property to the view and the call to create it. Our new struct's code is in Figure 11-5.

```
struct NotePriorityAndTime: View {
    var noteVM : NoteViewModel

    var body: some View {
        HStack {
            ForEach(noteVM.priorityImages, id: \.self)
            { (imageName) in
                Image(systemName: imageName)
                    .foregroundColor(self.noteVM.renderingColor)
            }
            Spacer()
            Text(noteVM.time)
                .fontWeight(.thin)
                .foregroundColor(self.noteVM.renderingColor)
        }
    }
}
```

Figure 11-5. NotePriorityAndTime View Struct

Remember to update the creation with the new noteVM parameter back in NoteRow's VStack.

```
NotePriorityAndTime(noteVM: noteVM)
```

If you run the app now, it should look the same as before. Also, we now have a new View we can include in our NoteView UI. You may want to create a new file for this View depending on how you choose to organize your code.

In NoteView, let's replace the current HStack code.

```
HStack {
    Spacer()
    Text("Updated At: \(noteVM.time)")
}
```

We can replace the entire HStack with the new View we created.

```
NotePriorityAndTime(noteVM: noteVM)
```

Where we had just the time before, we now have the priority and time using the rendering color as in Figure 11-6.

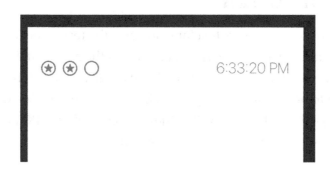

Figure 11-6. *NotePriorityAndTime in NoteView Preview*

If we run the app and tap on a row, we see the details of the note. It includes the priority and time now with the text and image as in Figure 11-7.

Figure 11-7. *Current Note Detail UI*

This might be OK for displaying the details, but it's not great. And it doesn't allow for editing the note. Let's get back to UIViewRepresentable to use a UITextView for the note text.

UIView in SwiftUI

Our current NoteView uses a Text for displaying the text of the note view model. That doesn't allow the user to edit text in the app. Swift has a TextEditor for that purpose. However, it's only available in iOS 14.

In order to be backward compatible, let's use a solution that will work in iOS 13 as well. We'll use the UITextView. Since that's in UIKit, we can use UIViewRepresentable and wrap it in a View struct.

UITEXTVIEW IN SWIFTUI

In order to use UIView subclasses in SwiftUI, we need to use UIViewRepresentable. So we'll create a new struct that conforms to that protocol.

1. Create a new TextView struct (this can be in the same file as NoteView or another file).

   ```
   struct TextView: UIViewRepresentable {}
   ```

2. Create a @Binding property for the text to be displayed.

   ```
   struct TextView: UIViewRepresentable {
       @Binding var text: String
   }
   ```

3. Implement the makeUIView function to return the UITextView.

   ```
   func makeUIView(context: Context) -> UITextView {
       return UITextView()
   }
   ```

Optionally, we can set other properties on the text view before returning it: font, colors, and so on.

4. Implement the updateUIView to update the UI if the text property is updated outside the struct.

```
func updateUIView(_ tvNote: UITextView,
    context: Context) {
        tvNote.text = text
}
```

5. Replace the Text item in the NoteView body with TextView.

```
TextView(text: $noteVM.text)
```

6. Preview or run the app and see that the UI appears the same as Figure 11-8.

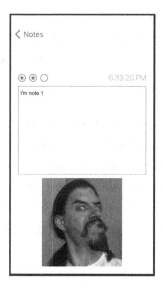

Figure 11-8. *NoteView with UITextView*

In this exercise, we added a UITextView to our SwiftUI. By creating a new struct that implements UIViewRepresentable, we wrapped our UIView in a View. By implementing the protocol, we provided the UIView (i.e., UITextView) and also updated the UI when the value might change.

You may notice that you can also edit the text in the text view. However, the changes aren't reflected in the previous view. That's because we're using a binding property wrapper in the NoteRow. Because of that, changes don't invalidate that UI to get recreated. We'll update that in the next chapter.

Chapter Summary

In some cases, you may need to use UIKit objects. This ability is provided by UIViewRepresentable in SwiftUI.

By implementing the protocol in a struct, you can implement methods to provide UIViews as a View object. The makeUIView function is called when the UIView needs to be created. If a binding value is changed, the updateUIView function is called.

Optionally, you can implement the dismantleUIView to clean up when the UIView will be removed from the user interface.

We also practiced extracting a view from an existing code.

Hopefully, you can see that whether you have existing views to use or need a UIKit view, you can easily do that in SwiftUI.

We'll look at more ways to work with SwiftUI using existing classes going forward.

CHAPTER 12

Data from UIKit with Coordinator

In the last chapter, we saw how to use a UIView in SwiftUI. In our project, we used the UITextView. Views like that allow the app to display text. However, it also allows users to edit text the app needs to know about.

UIKit provides various options for getting user data from the UI. In some cases, controls use events with the target/action pattern. In other cases, like text view, we also have mechanisms with the delegate pattern.

The last chapter showed us how to display information. In this chapter, we'll look at ways of getting user input from UIKit controls into SwiftUI code.

UIViewPresentable Protocol

You may have noticed a couple other things when we looked at the UIViewPresentable protocol in the last chapter. If we look again, we see mention of a Coordinator and function to create it as in Figure 12-1.

© Bear Cahill 2021
B. Cahill, *UI Design for iOS App Development*,
https://doi.org/10.1007/978-1-4842-6449-2_12

```
    /// A type to coordinate with the view.
    associatedtype Coordinator = Void
```

```
    /// SwiftUI calls this method before calling the
    ///   UIViewRepresentable/makeUIView(context:)   method. The system provides
    /// your coordinator either directly or as part of a context structure when
    /// calling the other methods of your representable instance.
    func makeCoordinator() -> Self.Coordinator
```

Figure 12-1. *Coordinator and makeCoordinator in UIViewPresentable*

The definition of makeCoordinator returns a Self.Coordinator. You can see above that code that Coordinator is type aliased to Void. However, in our code, we'll define an actual Coordinator class. Our implementation of the makeCoordinator function will return our defined type.

Coordinator

The coordinator is used to implement common patterns you may be familiar with in UIKit. It coordinates between the UIViews and SwiftUI. By using a coordinator, we can employ the delegate, datasource, and target/action patterns from UIKit.

So what do we need our coordinator to do? In our ListProject app, we are using a UITextView. We need to know when the user changes the text in the text view. For that, we can use the delegate of the UITextView.

Typically, you'd make the delegate assigned to your ViewController and implement UITextViewDelegate. Then your controller could implement the textViewDidChange function and access the text property.

In SwiftUI, we'll make our coordinator the delegate. That means our new Coordinator class needs to conform to that delegate and implement the textViewDidChange (and possibly others) function.

The declaration of our class could look something like this:

```
class Coordinator: UITextViewDelegate {...}
```

Note   I defined my Coordinator as a class **inside** the TextView struct.

If we add this, we immediately get an error. UITextViewDelegate inherits from UIScrollViewDelegate which inherits from NSObjectProtocol. Our Coordinator doesn't conform to NSObjectProtocol.

We can either add a ton of code to conform to NSObjectProtocol or we can inherit from NSObject. Since our Coordinator doesn't inherit from another class, we'll choose the latter.

```
class Coordinator: NSObject, UITextViewDelegate {...}
```

Problem solved.

Binding Property Wrapper

Now our TextView has a coordinator. Our TextView instance has a binding to the text passed in. We need that String to be updated as the user types. That's the job of our coordinator.

As the delegate, the Coordinator will implement textViewDidChange and need to store the updated text. So our Coordinator class needs a binding to the text also.

```
@Binding var text: String
```

To ensure that the property is set, we need an initializer that takes the binding as a parameter. We've been dealing with Structs that get the automatic member-wise constructor. Not so with our Coordinator since it's a class.

However, the syntax for passing in a binding as a parameter is a bit different. The @Binding property wrapper is simply a struct with a generic. So our parameter type can be spelled out that way for our init.

```
init(text: Binding<String>) {...}
```

Our parameter now has the type Binding<String>, but our property is a String with a property wrapper. If we try to assign self.text, we'll get an error that we can't assign our parameter to a String.

As a property wrapper, the compiler synthesizes the backing stored property. So our "text" property has a backing stored property named "_text" which we can access.

```
init(text: Binding<String>) {
    _text = text
}
```

Our coordinator has a binding property, and it's set in the initializer. Since we claim to conform to UITextViewDelegate, we can implement the function(s) we're interested in: textViewDidChange. There we can set the property wrapper's wrapped value.

```
func textViewDidChange(_ textView: UITextView) {
    _text.wrappedValue = textView.text
}
```

When the text changes, we set the wrapped value of the property.

Coordinator as Delegate

Now we have a coordinator that does the job we want. We need to implement makeCoordinator. If we implement that, it will be called before makeUIView. The coordinator is set as a property on the Context passed to makeUIView. With access to our Coordinator instance, we can set it as our UITextView's delegate property.

172

```
func makeUIView(context: Context) -> UITextView {
    let tv = UITextView()
    tv.delegate = context.coordinator
    return tv
}
```

Note   The following return type is TextView.Coordinator because the Coordinator class is defined **inside** the TextView struct.

```
func makeCoordinator() -> TextView.Coordinator {
    Coordinator(text: $text)
}
```

The bottom line is that the Coordinator class we defined is the UITextView's delegate. The mechanism to create the coordinator is built-in with the makeCoordinator protocol function. The mechanism to access the created Coordinator is provided by the Context.

The Context also has properties for Transaction and Environment. The Transaction contains information about animations. The Environment contains the environment variables. This way, your UIView can have access to values just like SwiftUI.

Alternate Syntax

If accessing the backing stored property doesn't feel right, that's OK. There's another way to pass in and access the property. Instead of using the @Binding syntax for the text property, we can use the same syntax as the init parameter.

```
class Coordinator: NSObject, UITextViewDelegate {
    var text: Binding<String>
```

173

Then the initializer and textViewDidChange can use the property more directly.

```
init(text: Binding<String>) {
    self.text = text
}

func textViewDidChange(_ textView: UITextView) {
    text.wrappedValue = textView.text
}
```

Our TextView doesn't have to vary in either case. Either way works, but now the code feels a bit cleaner. Let's use this version in an exercise now.

COORDINATOR FOR TEXTVIEW

We are going to add a coordinator to our TextView. It will be the delegate for the UITextView we create. The Coordinator will be a separate class and instantiated in the makeCoordinator protocol function.

Note If you've been updating your code as you follow along, you've already completed this exercise. Otherwise, the following steps spell out the changes necessary for the TextView's Coordinator.

---

1. Declare the Coordinator class inside TextView to inherit from NSObject and conform to UITextViewDelegate.

    ```
    class Coordinator: NSObject, UITextViewDelegate {}
    ```

2. Add the text property as a Binding<String> to the Coordinator.

    ```
    class Coordinator: NSObject, UITextViewDelegate {
        var text: Binding<String>
    }
    ```

3. Implement an initializer in the Coordinator that takes a Binding<String> parameter and sets it to the class property.

```
init(text: Binding<String>) {
    self.text = text
}
```

4. Implement the textViewDidChange in the Coordinator to set the wrapped value.

```
func textViewDidChange(_ textView: UITextView) {
    text.wrappedValue = textView.text
}
```

5. Implement makeCoordinator in the TextView class.

```
func makeCoordinator() -> TextView.Coordinator {
    Coordinator(text: $text)
}
```

6. Set the coordinator from the context as the created UITextView's delegate.

```
func makeUIView(context: Context) -> UITextView {
    let tv = UITextView()
    tv.delegate = context.coordinator
    return tv
}
```

The entire TextView struct code should look like Figure 12-2.

```
struct TextView: UIViewRepresentable {
    @Binding var text: String

    func makeUIView(context: Context) -> UITextView {
        let tv = UITextView()
        tv.delegate = context.coordinator
        return tv
    }

    func updateUIView(_ tvNote: UITextView, context: Context) {
        tvNote.text = text
    }

    func makeCoordinator() -> TextView.Coordinator {
        Coordinator(text: $text)
    }

    class Coordinator: NSObject, UITextViewDelegate {
        var text: Binding<String>

        init(text: Binding<String>) {
            self.text = text
        }

        func textViewDidChange(_ textView: UITextView) {
            text.wrappedValue = textView.text
        }
    }
}
```

Figure 12-2. *TextView with a Coordinator Class*

7. Run the app and verify, with breakpoints, that each function is called and the text is updated.

Now your UI is updating the TextView via the coordinator when the text changes. We're storing that value in the bound property which propagates back to the source of truth.

Updating the List

As noted in the previous chapter, the List isn't updating the rows with the edited values. In our ContentView's List, we aren't passing the note items to a binding property wrapper.

We can change the NoteRow to have a @Binding attribute for the noteVM property. However, that's going to break the code in various places. No worries. We can do it.

There's mainly just two changes. The first is to add @Binding to the NoteRow property.

```
struct NoteRow: View {
    @Binding var noteVM : NoteViewModel
```

This will break the preview of the NoteRow. You'll need to update that code to pass in a bound property also. It can mimic the way ContentView ForEach now uses the indices as in Figure 12-3.

```
struct NoteRow_Previews: PreviewProvider {
    @State private static var items = NoteViewModel.loadTestData()

    static var previews: some View {
        List {
            ForEach(items.indices) { (noteIndex) in
                NoteRow(noteVM: self.$items[noteIndex])
            }
        }
    }
}
```

Figure 12-3. *NoteRow Preview Updated*

Notice that the NoteRow is now created with a self.$items value. This binding is what we also need in the List in ContentView.

In the List for ContentView, we need to pass in a binding when it's created in the List. We simply put a $ in front of the item where we create the NoteRow.

```
NoteRow(noteVM: self.$items[noteIndex])
```

177

Now when we run the app and edit a note, it will be reflected in the List as in Figure 12-4.

Figure 12-4. *Updated Note*

Chapter Summary

Using the Coordinator mechanism from the UIViewRepresentable protocol, we now can edit a note. The change is reflected in the main ContentView's List also.

The coordinator concept is baked into the protocol and the Context passed into the related functions. However, the class we create can do what we need. In our case, it needed to conform to the UITextViewDelegate. That also requires the NSObjectProtocol so we inherited from NSObject.

We needed the text property for binding, but we could do other properties binding or not. We could also implement other protocols or use the class as a delegate or datasource of other UIView instances.

For our uses, we're just playing by the rules. We made the coordinate when we needed to, set it as the delegate, and handled the text changes.

You might be wondering, like I was, what if just create a Coordinator instance in makeUIView and set it as the delegate? Can that work? Yes and no.

The problem is the text view's delegate property is weak. That means it will immediately get released after the makeUIView call returns.

What if I make the coordinator a property of TextView? Yes, but you can't instantiate it in the declaration because it needs the text property.

What if I make it an optional property and instantiate it in the makeUIView? OK, but then you're mutating a member of the self. And if you mark makeUIView as mutating, you break the conformation to UIViewRepresentable.

What if I make the Coordinator a variable outside of TextView – maybe global or similar? Yes, that will work. It's a long way around the process, but it works. And if you want to pass in a Coordinator, maybe that's the way to go.

It does show an interesting point: the Coordinator setup as we used it isn't really required. It can be done other ways. However, the coordinator functions are there to help. Also, anyone familiar with the UIViewRepresentable may expect that route.

Now that we've seen the delegate pattern from UIKit used, we'll look at the target/action pattern next.

CHAPTER 13

Target/Action in SwiftUI

In the previous chapter, we used a Coordinator as our delegate for a UITextView. But we also realized the coordinator setup is just a helpful mechanism.

We could have made a new class for the delegate. Or we could have made the coordinate implement more protocols. The class we named Coordinate could have been named something else. I can inherit from another class and can implement what we need.

So can we use this same mechanism for the target/action pattern? Yes.

If you have an existing UIView, we've already seen you can use it with the UIViewRepresentable protocol. Declare its properties as usual (possibly binding). Implement the makeUIView to create your UIView instance and return it. Implement updateUIView to update the UI as necessary.

If you need a coordinator, implement makeCoordinator to return an instance of your coordinator class. It will get pass around in the Context as the coordinator property.

Overall, I'd say it's a good idea to keep the class name as Coordinator. My point is that the concept is what's important – not so much the specific name, parent class, or protocol of your coordinator class.

© Bear Cahill 2021
B. Cahill, *UI Design for iOS App Development*,
https://doi.org/10.1007/978-1-4842-6449-2_13

I've updated the code quite a bit. Nothing too interesting but you might want to start with the code base for this chapter. The concepts are the same. However, I moved some things into their own methods. This will help with reuse and UI updating. I'll review the key changes in the following.

Let's look at using the target/action pattern and the coordinator.

Target/Action

If you've ever created UIKit buttons, sliders, switches, and other elements in code, you're probably familiar with the addTarget function. The only trick here is the coordinator will be the target for the action. That means the function to call will also be on the coordinator.

If you're thinking that's no trick, you're right. Whenever you add a target in Swift, you specify the instance, the selector, and the event. Nothing new here.

Again, there's nothing all that special here. We define a class. We return an instance of it from makeCoordinator. Walking through the code may make it feel complex, but the core setup is something you're probably already familiar with.

ButtonView

In the ListProject, I have a UIView subclass called ButtonView in NoteRow. swift. This will be our example of a view we're importing from existing code. The declaration and init look like Figure 13-1.

```
let buttonHW : CGFloat = 40

class ButtonView : UIView {
    var noteVM : NoteViewModel?

    init(rect : CGRect, noteVM : NoteViewModel) {
        super.init(frame: rect)
        self.noteVM = noteVM
        configUI()
    }
}
```

Figure 13-1. *ButtonView Declaration and Initializer*

We have a let constant for the button height and width, a
NoteViewModel property, and an initializer. The init calls a super init, sets
the property, and calls configUI (see Figure 13-2).

```
func configUI() {
    guard let nvm = self.noteVM else { return }
    let renderColor = nvm.renderingColor == .red ? UIColor.red : UIColor.label

    var btnRect = self.frame
    btnRect.size.width = buttonHW
    for btnIndex in 0..<3 {
        let btn = UIButton(type: .roundedRect)
        btnRect.origin.x = CGFloat(btnIndex) * buttonHW
        btn.frame = btnRect
        btn.tintColor = renderColor
        btn.tag = btnIndex
        let img = UIImage(systemName: noteVM!.priorityImages[btnIndex])
        btn.setImage(img, for: .normal)
        self.addSubview(btn)
    }
}
```

Figure 13-2. *configUI Method*

This method loops through and creates three buttons based on the
priority images of the NoteViewModel property. It uses the loop index to
set the tag on the buttons. This will come in handy later when calculating
the new priority.

Typically, we would also add the target to the UIButton instances. However, we'll be using the Coordinator so that the code isn't in the preceding function.

There's also a required init for Storyboards. Since we aren't using those, it's just the boilerplate version as in Figure 13-3.

```
required init?(coder: NSCoder) {
    fatalError("init(coder:) has not been implemented")
}
```

Figure 13-3. Required Init (Not Used)

So we have our UIView we need to reuse in our SwiftUI code.

UIView in SwiftUI

As before, we'll create a struct that implements UIViewRepresentable. I named mine PriorityStarButtons. This struct will create the ButtonView in the makeUIView implementation. It will update the view as necessary in updateUIView.

It also needs a NoteViewModel to send to the ButtonView. The code in NoteRow.swift looks like Figure 13-4.

```swift
struct PriorityStarButtons : UIViewRepresentable {
    var noteVM : NoteViewModel

    init(noteViewModel : NoteViewModel) {
        noteVM = noteViewModel
    }

    func makeUIView(context: Context) -> UIView {
        let rect = CGRect(x: 0, y: 14, width: buttonHW*3, height: buttonHW)
        return ButtonView(rect: rect, noteVM: noteVM)
    }

    func updateUIView(_ uiView: UIView, context: Context) {
    }
}
```

Figure 13-4. *PriorityStarButtons Class*

Where we previously created the star images in a ForEach loop, we'll use this new class. So we can update NotePriorityAndTime in the same file to use our PriorityStarButtons as in Figure 13-5.

```swift
struct NotePriorityAndTime: View {
    @Binding var noteVM : NoteViewModel

    var body: some View {
        HStack {
            PriorityStarButtons(noteViewModel: self.noteVM)
            Spacer()
            Text(noteVM.time)
                .fontWeight(.thin)
                .foregroundColor(self.noteVM.renderingColor)
        }
    }
}
```

Figure 13-5. *NotePriorityAndTime Using PriorityStarButtons*

Running the app should still look similar but with a slight change to the star images. They're buttons now with a set size as in Figure 13-6.

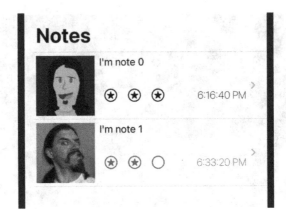

Figure 13-6. *UI Using PriorityStarButtons*

Adding the Coordinator

At this point, we're just wrapping the UIView in our new struct. We want to update the code to use the Coordinator for our button targets. On top of that, if the user taps a start button, we want to update the NoteViewModel.

Ideally, we'd like to propagate that change whether we're on the main list UI or the details of the note. That means we need to add binding.

Both the PriorityStarButtons struct and the ButtonView class have a NoteViewModel property. That can be changed to a binding type. Then accessing will require some code changes.

The PriorityStarButtons struct conforms to UIViewRepresentable. That's where we'll create the Coordinator. The Coordinator can then be passed into the ButtonsView to set up the target relationship for the buttons.

```
ACTION/TARGET IN SWIFT
```

In this exercise, we'll prep the new class and struct to handle bindings for the NoteViewModel. Then we can create the coordinator and pass it into the ButtonsView for the target. Finally, we'll handle the button tap in the coordinator to update the model. That will cause the UI to be updated as well.

1. In NoteRow.swift, change the PriorityStarButtons property to be a binding.

    ```
    var noteVM : Binding<NoteViewModel>
    ```

    The preceding change will cause a cascading of errors. To fix this, we will propagate the types of the properties being set and the parameters being passed.

2. Change the init for PriorityStarButtons to take the same type as the property changed in step 1.

    ```
    init(noteViewModel : Binding<NoteViewModel>) { noteVM =
        noteViewModel
    }
    ```

    Where we create the PriorityStarButtons instance, NotePriorityAndTime needs to be updated. Currently, it calls the init for PriorityStarButtons without the binding.

3. Change the PriorityStarButtons initialization call to pass in the note view model binding.

    ```
    PriorityStarButtons(noteViewModel: self.$noteVM)
    ```

4. In ButtonView, change the property and init parameter types.

    ```
    class ButtonView : UIView {
        var noteVM : Binding<NoteViewModel>?
        init(rect : CGRect,
            noteVM : Binding<NoteViewModel>)
    ```

187

That should fix the compile error caused earlier. Now we can move on to fix the new errors.

5. In configUI for ButtonView, access the wrapped value for the renderingColor.

```
let renderColor =
    nvm.renderingColor.wrappedValue
    == .red ? UIColor.red : UIColor.label
```

6. And access the wrapped value for the priorityImage array element.

```
let img = UIImage(systemName:
    noteVM!.priorityImages[btnIndex].wrappedValue)
```

At this point, we have basically the same things as before but with binding. The functionality shouldn't have changed. Run your app and make sure it still looks the same.

Now let's create our Coordinator. This new class could also take a binding to the NoteViewModel. However, for variation, we'll just use bindings for the specific values we care about: image strings and time string.

7. Within the PriorityStarButtons class, declare a new class for the coordinator. Include the two binding properties also.

```
class Coordinator : NSObject {
    var images : Binding<[String]>
    var time : Binding<String>
}
```

8. Create an initializer for the Coordinator class that takes the two
    values to be stored in the property bindings.

```
init(images : Binding<[String]>,
    time : Binding<String>) {
    self.images = images
    self.time = time
}
```

Since we know that the Coordinator class will be the target for our
buttons, we can implement the needed method now.

This function will need one parameter for the button. Also, it needs to
be exposed to Objective-C to be sent into the addTarget function.

The functionality of the method will update the bound values in the
properties of the Coordinator.

9. Create a function in the Coordinator for the event when the user
    taps a button.

```
@objc func priorityChange(sender : UIButton) {
    time.wrappedValue =
        NoteViewModel.dateFormatter.string(from: Date())
    let newPrority = Priority(rawValue: sender.tag)!
    images.wrappedValue =
        NoteViewModel.handlePriority(priority:
            newPrority)
}
```

We set the time wrapped value to a new string. We reuse the static
date formatter in NoteViewModel to create a current updated at time.

We use the UIButton tag value to create a new priority. Then we use
a new function on NoteViewModel to handle the new priority. This
recreates the image name strings based on the priority and returns

189

them. Having this in a separate method allows us to change the image name bindings outside of creating a new NoteViewModel.

10.   Create the Coordinator in makeCoordinator.

```
func makeCoordinator() -> Coordinator {
    return Coordinator(images:
        self.noteVM.priorityImages,
            time: self.noteVM.time)
}
```

Now that the noteVM property is a binding, we can pass in the values when creating the coordinator.

Currently, our ButtonView doesn't know anything about the Coordinator. When the ButtonView is created, it will need the Coordinator instance to add the target to the buttons.

11.   Add the coordinator to the creation of ButtonView in the makeUIView method.

```
return ButtonView(rect: rect,
                  noteVM: noteVM,
                  coordinator: context.coordinator)
```

Now we need to receive the coordinator in the ButtonView init and pass it into the configUI.

12.   Add the Coordinator parameter to the init and the call to configUI.

```
init(rect : CGRect, noteVM : Binding<NoteViewModel>,
    coordinator: PriorityStarButtons.Coordinator) {
    super.init(frame: rect)
    self.noteVM = noteVM
    configUI(coordinator: coordinator)
}
```

13.   Add the Coordinator as a parameter to configUI in ButtonView.

```
func configUI(coordinator:
  PriorityStarButtons.Coordinator) {...
```

14.   Set the target on the button to the coordinator using the
      selector we defined and the touchUpInside event.

```
btn.addTarget(coordinator,
  action: #selector(PriorityStarButtons
    .Coordinator.priorityChange(sender:)),
  for: .touchUpInside)
```

The only thing left is to implement the updateUIView. Its first
parameter is a UIView. We know this is the ButtonView, and we can
verify that with a guard statement.

Once we have the typecast ButtonView, we can update the
UI. However, we don't want to recreate the UI. Let's add a function to
ButtonView to update the button images based on the tag.

The tag can serve as the index in the image name string array. If the
image names have been properly updated, this will work fine.

15.   Create a function in ButtonView to update the button images.

```
func configPriorityImages() {
    subviews.forEach { (btn) in
        guard let btn = btn as? UIButton else
          { return }

        let imageIndex = btn.tag
        let imageName =
          noteVM!
          .priorityImages[imageIndex].wrappedValue
```

```
        let img = UIImage(systemName: imageName)
           btn.setImage(img, for: .normal)
        }
    }
```

This function, when called, loops through the subviews searching for UIButtons. It then gets the tag and uses that to get the image name from the priorityImages array. It creates an image from that name and sets it on the button.

Now we just need to call that function to update the UI when necessary.

16.   Update the UI in updateUIView.

```
func updateUIView(_ uiView: UIView,
                    context: Context) {
    guard let v = uiView as? ButtonView
        else { return }
    v.configPriorityImages()
}
```

This function verifies, with a guard statement, that the UIView is a ButtonView. Then it calls configPriorityImages on it.

That's a lot of work! We took an existing UIView (i.e., ButtonView) and wrapped in a struct named PriorityStarButtons which implements UIViewRepresentable.

That struct has a binding NoteViewModel which is set in its initializer. Its makeUIView function creates a CGRect and instantiates the ButtonView with the rect. It also passes in the NoteViewModel binding and coordinator from the context.

The ButtonView initializer stores the binding in noteVM and passes the coordinator into configUI. That call sets up the UI including adding the targets to the buttons for the Coordinator.

PriorityStarButtons creates the coordinator in makeCoordinator. It passes in the priority image names and the time – both from the NoteViewModel.

The Coordinator has two bindings: images (String Array) and time (String). Those are set in the initializer. It also has a function to call for a button action. This is added as a target to the existing buttons.

That target function updates the time and image names. That causes the UI to be updated which calls updateUIView. That in turn calls configPriorityImages which updates the images.

In short, PriorityStarButtons creates the ButtonView, gives it the model and coordinator, and tells ButtonView when to update.

ButtonView creates its buttons, adds the target to the coordinator, and updates the button images when told to.

Since we're using bindings to pass the data around, whether you change the priority in the List or the details screen, it's kept in sync.

If you run the app, it should update as you tap the buttons. And if you view the details, it should do the same. Also notice the time updates as in Figure 13-7.

Figure 13-7. *Current UI with Updated Time*

We did a lot in this exercise. But I hope you see the clear distinctions. The UIViewRepresentable struct creates and updates the UI as we saw before.

The Coordinator is a fairly open-ended class that gets created as part of the protocol functions. And it's passed around the Context. But other than that, it's pretty open-ended.

The main changes to our ButtonView were to change the property to a binding and add the target to the coordinator. Chances are if that UI was created in code, it would have already had the addTarget call. We just needed to change it.

Chapter Summary

In this chapter, we saw how to use an existing UIView. We wrapped it in a struct that conforms to UIViewRepresentable. We created it and updated it as part of the protocol functions.

We created a coordinator that had bindings and a function valid for an addTarget selector.

To keep ButtonView from having to know about the Coordinator, it could be passed in as a custom protocol defined in your code. Depending on your specific app requirements, there are various twists you can put on this concept.

There are a few main points I hope you take away. The UIViewRepresentable is responsible for creating and updating the UIView it manages. If bindings are needed, no problem. We're comfortable with those now.

A coordinator can be just about anything and can serve the purposes you need. It's created in the makeCoordinator. It's returned from that function and then passed around in the context.

Now we know how to use a UIView with the delegate and target/action patterns!

CHAPTER 14

SwiftUI in UIKit

We looked at how to use existing UIKit views in SwiftUI. Now we'll look at how to use SwiftUI in UIKit.

You may have an existing project that you want to add new UI using SwiftUI. So you have your Storyboard setup for all your interface and navigation. It's actually pretty easy to add SwiftUI views to your project.

When we incorporated a UIView in our app, we used UIViewRepresentable. That protocol facilitated creating our UIView instances.

UIKit provides a mechanism for doing it the other way around. There's a UIViewController subclass called UIHostingController. Similarly, for macOS development, there's NSHostingController. And the WatchKit version is named WKHostingController.

UIHostingController takes a SwiftUI View in the initializer. So you're responsible for creating your new SwiftUI View. You create the UIHostingController instance with that and present it.

In this chapter, we'll look at doing this including Storyboard incorporation.

UIHostingController

This new controller is included in the object library. That means it's easy to add to your existing Storyboard. It's listed in the object library along with the other controllers as in Figure 14-1.

© Bear Cahill 2021
B. Cahill, *UI Design for iOS App Development*,
https://doi.org/10.1007/978-1-4842-6449-2_14

Figure 14-1. *Hosting View Controller in the Object Library*

Updating the Storyboard with this view controller is the same as any other. Just drag one from the object library to your Storyboard in Interface Builder.

Creating a segue to this new controller is the same too. Just control-drag from a button or table view to your new view controller. It fits right in like any other view controller as in Figure 14-2.

Figure 14-2. *Segue from the Table Cell to Hosting Controller in the Storyboard*

Xcode allows you to control-drag from the Storyboard into the source view controller's code. This creates an IBSegueAction called when the segue fires. The segue action has a return type that expects a view controller.

```
@IBSegueAction func showDetails(_ coder: NSCoder)
        -> UIViewController? {
    return UIHostingController(coder: coder,
        rootView: swiftUIView)
}
```

The return type of your generated code may have a return type not set to UIViewController. If so, you'll need to change that to UIViewController.

In the implementation, you need to create an instance of UIHostingController. You pass in the coder that was sent to the function being called. The second parameter is your new SwiftUI view.

The preceding code only shows the creation of the UIHostingController with a placeholder of SwiftUI view. Depending on the view you design, the instantiation of it will vary.

ADDING A SWIFTUI VIEW TO UIKIT

Let's start with a basic exercise. We'll create a simple Storyboard app and add a SwiftUI view.

1. Create a new iOS App template project using the Storyboard and name it Simple14 as in Figure 14-3.

Figure 14-3. *New iOS App Project with the Storyboard Interface*

2.   Add a button to your initial view controller from the Object Library.

3.   Drag a Hosting View Controller from the Object Library onto your Storyboard to the right of the initial view controller.

4.   Control-drag from the button to your Hosting View Controller.

When you release over the Hosting View Controller, select "Show" at the top of the segue options pop-up menu.

Your UI in the Storyboard should look like Figure 14-4.

Figure 14-4. *Segue from the Initial View Controller to Hosting Controller in the Storyboard*

Next, we need to create the segue action into the code.

5. Open the assistant (Editor ➤ Assistant or ⌃⌥⌘↩) to display the ViewController code to the right.

6. Control-drag from the segue into your ViewController code above the last closing curly brace (}) and release.

7. In the resulting pop-up, give your segue action function a name (e.g., showSwiftUI) as in Figure 14-5.

199

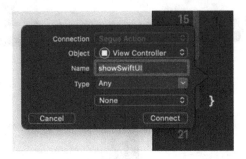

Figure 14-5. *Naming the Segue Action*

8. Click the Connect button and review the generated code.

    At this point, we're done with the Storyboard and can close that. Next, we need to create our SwiftUI view to have something to display.

9. Add a new file to your project (⌘+n) – select the "SwiftUI View" type and click Next.

10. Name the file MySwiftUI and click Create.

    The preview won't work because there's a compile error. Our segue action isn't implemented. Let's fix it now back in the ViewController class.

11. Open ViewController.swift and import SwiftUI above the declaration of your ViewController class.

    ```
    import SwiftUI
    ```

12. Implement the showSwiftUI function to return an instance of UIHostingController. Pass in the code and an instance of your new MySwiftUI struct.

    ```
    @IBSegueAction func showSwiftUI(_ coder: NSCoder)
            -> UIViewController? {
        return UIHostingController(coder: coder,
            rootView: MySwiftUI())
    }
    ```

13.   Run the app and tap the button. The SwiftUI view should display like Figure 14-6.

Figure 14-6. MySwiftUIView Displayed in the Simulator

Congrats! You've incorporated a SwiftUI view into a UIKit/Storyboard app.

For a simple project, that was easy, right? It's not much more for complicated projects. It really depends on the SwiftUI view you create. If it needs interaction or data, there's more to it.

Next, we're going to look at doing something like that.

Existing Project

I've provided a Begin of Chapter (BOC) project for you: Ch14_BOC_ Timers.zip. This project allows the user to create timers. A timer has a name and amount of time. The user can start and pause a timer.

When a timer runs out, it pops up a local notification assuming the user gave the authorization to the app.

Swiping to the right gives the option to remove a timer. Right swiping displays the start/pause button as in Figure 14-7.

Figure 14-7. *Starting a Timer with Right Swipe*

The + button allows the user to create new timers. The code has some test timers created automatically for debug builds.

This is our starting point. However, we want to add UI using SwiftUI. When a user taps on a timer in the list, we want to show details. The simple UI of the details will include the name, time, and Start/Pause button.

Also, the UI should update as the seconds tick away for the timer.

Adding SwiftUI

As we did in the previous exercise, we need to add a Hosting View Controller to our Storyboard. Then we create the segue action into the code: TimerListVC. In this case, we'll do it from the table view cell.

Again, as in the last exercise, that's all we'll do in the Storyboard.

The segue action function generated needs a UIViewController returned. Once again, like before, we'll create an instance of our SwiftUI view. That and the code passed in will be used to create the Hosting View Controller to return. So we need a SwiftUI view to create!

We've seen before how our View struct gets a member-wise initializer. In the case of the Timers project, that will include the TimerItem for the details to display.

The two nonobvious parts are updating the UI for the time and the button to start/pause the timer. And those aren't tricky at all.

ADDING TIMER VIEW TO UIKIT

Open the provided BOC project, Ch14_BOC_Timers.zip, and navigate to the Storyboard.

1. Add a Hosting View Controller to the Storyboard from the Object Library.

2. Control-drag from the table view cell to the new Hosting View Controller, release, and select Show from the pop-up menu.

Your Storyboard should look like Figure 14-8.

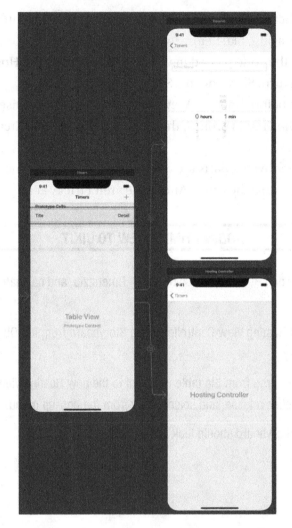

Figure 14-8. *Storyboard with Hosting View Controller and Segue*

3.   Open the Assistant (Editor ➤ Assistant or ^⌥⌘↵).

4.   Control-drag from the segue into the TimerListVC.swift code (below the makeTimer function), release, and name the function timerDetails.

Now we need to create our TimerView to display our timer details.

5. Add a new SwiftUI View file to your project named TimerView.
    swift.

    We'll replace the body property contents with the Timer details.
    Of course, we need a TimerItem for the details.

6. Add the TimerItem property and body contents.

```
struct TimerView: View {
    var timer : TimerItem
    var body: some View {
        VStack {
            Text(timer.name)
            Text(timer.timeString)
        }
    }
}
```

7. Update the TimerView_Previews to pass in a TimerItem.

```
struct TimerView_Previews: PreviewProvider {
    static var timer = TimerItem(name: "Test Timer",
            seconds: 12)

    static var previews: some View {
        TimerView(timer: timer)
    }
}
```

The preview won't display because we have an error back
where we need to create the UIHostingController in TimerListVC.
swift.

Now we can create this in our segue action back in TimerListVC
and display it.

This segue is called when the user selects a row in the table view.
That means we can get that row number from the table view.

205

8.   Create a let to store the TimerItem from the array and assign it using the selected row.

```
@IBSegueAction func timerDetails(_ coder: NSCoder)
    -> UIViewController? {
let timer =
    timers[tableView.indexPathForSelectedRow!.row]
```

9.   Create the TimerView instance using the timer from the array.

```
let tView = TimerView(timer: timer)
```

10.   Return the UIHostingController instance created with the coder and tView created (the whole function is as follows).

```
@IBSegueAction func timerDetails(_ coder: NSCoder)
    -> UIViewController? {
let timer =
    timers[tableView.indexPathForSelectedRow!.row]
let tView = TimerView(timer: timer)
return UIHostingController(coder: coder,
                          rootView: tView)
}
```

Now that we've added the UIHostingController code, we need SwiftUI. So we need to import SwiftUI.

11.   Uncomment out the SwiftUI import at the top of the file.

Running the app now displays the details when a row is tapped. The UI is very basic (see Figure 14-9), but that's what we designed.

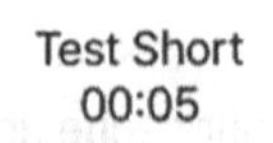

Test Short
00:05

Figure 14-9. *MySwiftUIView in the Simulator*

That was easy, right? We just added the Hosting View Controller and created the segue action for our Storyboard. We designed a simple SwiftUI View, created it with a timer, and returned the UIHostingController.

Passing ObservableObject

You may remember we wanted to have the timer update on the SwiftUI view. Also, we want a Start/Pause button. If you run the app, you'll notice the timer doesn't update in our new view.

In some of our exercises, we used binding to solve this type of challenge. But our model in TimerListVC is TimerItem instances. If we changed that to some type of binding, a lot of code would have to change.

Binding only works on value types (structs, enums), and our TimerItem is a reference type (class).

Changing the TimerItem to a struct for binding could have a lot of implications in our code. Some code may rely on passing the reference around for changes.

We'll keep it as a class. The ObservableObject protocol is made for reference types so we'll use that.

MAKING TIMER ITEM OBSERVABLE

We only need a few changes for this. We have to declare TimerItem conforms to ObservableObject. With that, we can declare what property or properties to publish with the @Published wrapper. And we need to tell the code when to send changes.

The TimerView also needs to be updated to mark the property as an ObservedObject. We can also update the UI with the Start/Pause button.

1. Open the TimerItem.swift code and declare it implements the ObservableObject protocol.

    ```
    class TimerItem : ObservableObject {
    ```

2. Mark the timeString property as published.

    ```
    @Published var timeString = ""
    ```

3. In the start function, at the top of the scheduled timer closure (e.g., line 69), add the send function call.

    ```
    self.objectWillChange.send()
    ```

    Now that the TimerItem is observable, we can declare that in the TimerView.

4. In TimerView, declare the timer property as an observed object.

    ```
    @ObservedObject var timer : TimerItem
    ```

    At this point, the timer duration will update in the TimerView. However, you have to start the timer in the table view before viewing its details.

    Let's add the Start/Pause button in our TimerView. We can add that under the two text items. The Button needs an action and what to display for the visual part of the button.

    The action can check the isRunning property on the timer. If it's running, it can pause the timer. Otherwise, it can start the timer.

    For the label parameter, we can use a Text element.

5. In TimerView, add a Button below the two Text items. For the action, check the isRunning parameter and pause or start the timer based on its setting. For the label, create a Text element.

```
Button(action: {
    if self.timer.isRunning {
        self.timer.pause()
    }
    else {
        self.timer.start()
    }
}) {
    Text(timer.isRunning ? "Pause" : "Start")
}
```

Just to make it a little more formatted, let's add a couple modifiers to the timer displaying the remaining duration.

6. On the second text item, for timer.timeString, add font and padding modifiers.

```
Text(timer.timeString)
    .font(.largeTitle)
    .padding()
```

Now viewing a timer's details allows us to start/pause the timer. When started, we can see the timer count down the remaining time as in Figure 14-10.

Test 3

11:54

Pause

Figure 14-10. Timer Details UI with Button and Time Remaining

Notice that when you tap Pause, it doesn't update to Start. Why do you think that is? The pause function in TimerItem invalidates the timer. But the timer's closure is when we publish the changes.

This can be fixed in two ways: send the updates out in the pause function or mark the isRunning property with @Published. Try those out.

To add the ability to update our UI with changes didn't take too many changes. We had to specify the TimerItem was an ObservableObject. Then we had to mark the timeString as published and call the send function.

With those changes, we just had to specify the property in TimerView as an observed object. We also added the Start/Pause button and modifiers to a Text item.

Chapter Summary

In this chapter, we focused on using SwiftUI views in an existing Storyboard-based project. The provided Hosting View Controller and segue action allowed for this to be easy.

With the Hosting View Controller in our Storyboard and a segue, we created the segue action in our code. That gets passed a coder. We needed to create our SwiftUI view instance. With the coder and our view, we created the Hosting View Controller and returned it from the segue action.

Notice that we created the view controller to return. That means we have access to set other properties on our view or the view controller in one place. There's no need to implement the prepare for segue function.

To allow the SwiftUI to update dynamically, it needed a couple more changes. We chose to use the ObservableObject protocol since our TimerItem was a reference type (class).

We declared it implements the protocol, specified the published property, and called the send function when necessary.

The only thing left was to mark the TimerView property as an observed object.

In our first exercise in this chapter, we saw that it takes very little work to display SwiftUI in a UIKit project. The second exercise shows even UI updates and interaction don't take much.

This methodology allows for existing projects to benefit seamlessly from new SwiftUI user interface development.

CHAPTER 15

Introduction to Combine

We've already been using the Combine framework a good bit. Now we're going to pause on SwiftUI and look a bit more closely at Combine.

Apple describes the framework as "a unified, declarative API for processing values over time." The part I want to focus on is the "processing values over time."

That's how we've been using Combine so far. As our values have changed over time, our UI has updated. We used @State, @Binding, @Published, and more.

Using these wrappers in SwiftUI has really facilitated changes reflected in our UI. But it can be easy to confuse these Combine framework aspects with SwiftUI.

The Combine framework can be used without SwiftUI. This can help your existing apps even without using SwiftUI. Understanding this framework will improve your apps across the board. Also, it will set you up to set the stage for adding SwiftUI as you update your current apps.

Common Concepts

Apps are built using the basic concept of displaying an interface to the user. The user's input is stored in the app, and the functionality is driven by these actions and data. We know this.

© Bear Cahill 2021
B. Cahill, *UI Design for iOS App Development*,
https://doi.org/10.1007/978-1-4842-6449-2_15

So it's a common paradigm to store the user's text input in a String property. Similarly, we may display that data or a version of it after some functionality.

Let's look at a simple example.

Let's say we have a basic UI design of a textfield and label. We have outlets to them in our view controller. There's also an action on the textfield for editingChanged. That function stores the entered text and puts it in the label. The code is in Figure 15-1.

```swift
import UIKit

class ViewController: UIViewController {

    @IBOutlet weak var tf: UITextField!
    @IBOutlet weak var lbl: UILabel!
    var userText : String?

    @IBAction func textChange(sender : UITextField) {
        userText = sender.text
        lbl.text = userText
    }

}
```

Figure 15-1. *Basic UI ViewController Code to Update a Label with TextField Changes*

If you run this app, the label will update as you type in the textfield. Let's look at a way to do this using Combine framework concepts.

Publisher and Subscriber

Combine uses the concepts of publisher and subscriber. You may be familiar with the NotificationCenter. It can post notifications. Any observers added for that notification name get notified by calling the associated function.

The publisher defines its specific output type. The output is the value it sends when it publishes. The subscriber defines its specific input type. The type it receives from publishers. These types must match. Later, we'll look at ways to map the values when they don't match.

Both the publisher and subscriber each define a failure type. The failure types must also match to set up the relationship.

There are multiple ways to create a publisher. The first one we'll look at uses the NotificationCenter. This is a familiar dynamic to many so it's a good place to start.

Once we have a publisher, we can add a subscriber to it. This will handle the data when it's published.

CONVERTING TO COMBINE

This example won't necessarily do this more efficiently nor will it be less code. It will be more code actually. However, the purpose is to take a familiar concept and show how it would work in a new concept.

First, we need to import the Combine framework into our code. Then we want to get a publisher from the NotificationCenter. We are going to subscribe our ViewController to the updates so it needs to confirm to the Subscriber. It, of course, needs to implement the various requirements.

Within the implementation of the Subscriber, we'll get the new text value entered and update the UI.

I have provided a Ch15_BOC_CombineFW.zip file with the starting point of this code. It is simply the code discussed earlier in this chapter.

1. Import the Combine framework into the code.

```
import Combine
```

2. Get a publisher from the NotificationCenter in viewDidLoad.

```
let publisher = NotificationCenter
    .default
    .publisher(for:
            UITextField.textDidChangeNotification,
            object: tf)
```

This returns a publisher for the textfield. It will publish whenever the text changes in that field.

3. Subscribe the ViewController to the publisher. Since we're updating the UI, we want to receive the updates on the main thread.

```
publisher
    .receive(on: DispatchQueue.main)
    .subscribe(self)
```

Alternatively, you could subscribe on the main thread and call receive with the subscriber. I like the code above because of the clarity: I want to receive on the main thread (for the UI) and subscribe the given instance passed in.

At this point, we have the publisher and have subscribed. Sort of. Our ViewController doesn't implement a Subscriber.

4. Add Subscriber to the declaration.

```
class ViewController: UIViewController, Subscriber {
```

5. Use the Fix button in the compilation error message to stub out the code. It will likely only add the type type aliases need: Input and Failure.

```
typealias Input = type
typealias Failure = type
```

We need to know what to set these to. If we drill down into the
.publisher call, we see it returns a NotificationCenter.Publisher.
If we navigate to that (it's just below the publisher function
declaration), we see the output is Notification and failure is
Never.

Our Input and Failure need to match those.

```
typealias Input = Notification
typealias Failure = Never
```

We still have a compile error. If we use the Fix button again, it stubs
out the functions we need.

6. Implement the receive subscription function to specify unlimited
    updates of the data.

```
func receive(subscription: Subscription) {
    subscription.request(.unlimited)
}
```

7. Implement the receive input function.

```
func receive(_ input: Input) -> Subscribers.Demand {
    if let textField = input.object as? UITextField {
        userText = textField.text
        lbl.text = userText
    }

    return .unlimited
}
```

Since our Input type alias specified it is a Notification, we can
use it that way. We're on the UI thread so updates work fine.

Return .unlimited indicating that we want to continue with
unlimited responses.

8. Implement the receive completion function.

```
func receive(completion:
    Subscribers.Completion<Failure>) {
        print(completion)
}
```

There's nothing we need to do in our case, but in some cases, you may want to finalize something in your app at this point.

At this point, we have our ViewController subscribed to the NotificationCenter updates for our textfield. If we run the app, as we type in the textfield, the label should be updated. The UI should look like Figure 15-2.

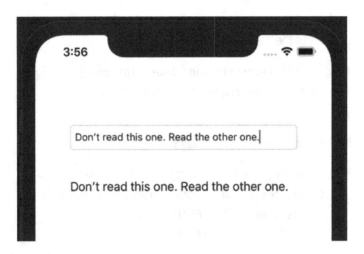

Figure 15-2. *TextField Input Set as the Label Text*

As I'm sure you agree, this was more work, code, and complexity than the original solution. But, again, this example was to walk us through the concepts of publisher and subscriber from the Combine framework. More refinement is coming next.

The solution is stored in CombineFW-Ex15-1.zip.

Refinements

One easy change we could make to our code is to chain the subscribe call to the publisher call in viewDidLoad.

```
NotificationCenter
    .default
    .publisher(for:
              UITextField.textDidChangeNotification,
              object: tf)
    .receive(on: DispatchQueue.main)
    .subscribe(self)
```

Now we don't need to store the publisher at all. But it gets even better!

Combine provides two subscribers we can use instead of our own class. They automatically match the output and failure types to the publisher they are attached to. What is this magic? Sink and assign.

Sink Subscriber

The sink subscriber takes two closures. The first is called just like our receive completion function we wrote. The second closure is just like the function we wrote to take the updated value. That updated value in our case is a Notification instance.

Sink automatically requests unlimited number of updates as we did in our receive subscription function. And when Combine creates your subscriber, it uses the thread the change occurred on. In our case, the change is in the UI so it's already on the main thread.

If we use sink, we can remove the calls to receive and subscribe. However, sink has a return value we need to consider. It returns an AnyCancellable.

We can store this in a class property. We don't want it to go out of scope and get removed from memory. If we want to cancel the subscription, we call .cancel on this value. Once it's out of scope, it will get cleaned up, and .cancel will be called automatically in its deinit. Clean.

So we need a property.

```
var subscriber : AnyCancellable?
```

And we can use it when we create our publisher and subscriber.

```
subscriber = NotificationCenter
    .default
    .publisher(for:
            UITextField.textDidChangeNotification,
            object: tf)
    .sink(receiveCompletion: { print ($0) })
        { (notification) in
            if let textField = notification.object
                            as? UITextField {
                self.userText = textField.text
                self.lbl.text = self.userText
            }
        }
```

We get the publisher as we did before. Now we're calling sink on it. Our receiveCompletion closure just prints out the parameter. Our updated value closure does the same as before (but with added self-scoping for the properties).

Best of all, our ViewController doesn't have to be a Subscriber, and we can remove all of that code! Suddenly our entire code base got a lot smaller as in Figure 15-3 (especially if we remove the connection from our textfield in the Storyboard as I have done).

```
import UIKit
import Combine

class ViewController: UIViewController {
    @IBOutlet weak var tf: UITextField!
    @IBOutlet weak var lbl: UILabel!
    var userText : String?
    var subscriber : AnyCancellable?

    override func viewDidLoad() {
        super.viewDidLoad()

    subscriber = NotificationCenter
        .default
        .publisher(for: UITextField.textDidChangeNotification,
                object: tf)
        .sink(receiveCompletion: { print ($0) })
            { (notification) in
                if let textField = notification.object as? UITextField {
                    self.userText = textField.text
                    self.lbl.text = self.userText
                }
            }
    }
}
```

Figure 15-3. *ViewController Without Subscriber Protocol and with Sink*

Sink also has a version that doesn't take a completion closure. So if you don't need that, your code can get even smaller.

Assign Subscriber

The second provided subscriber from Combine is assign. Assign takes two parameters. The first is a key path to a property. The second is an instance with that key path.

In the case of our project, the key path is for the text element of the UILabel. Of course, the second parameter is the label itself. Instead of sink, we can use assign to make the assignment to our property.

```
.assign(to: \.userText, on: self)
```

Now our subscriber receives the published value and assigns it to the userText property. One problem, our published value is a notification and not a String.

To get to the String value, we have to get the object out of the notification. The object is the UITextField, and from that we can get the text. We need an intermediate step.

Operators

Fortunately for us, Publisher in Combine has a lot of operators. If you're familiar with the standard higher-order functions, you'll feel at home.

Publisher provides many operators like map, flatMap, reduce, contains, and more. You can see a long list of them in the Apple documentation for Publisher (https://developer.apple.com/documentation/combine/publisher).

On our publisher, we can add a map to drill down into the Notification to get what we need.

```
.map { notif in
    guard let tf = notif.object as? UITextField
        else { return "" }
    return tf.text
}
.assign(to: \.userText, on: self)
```

Now when the value is published, we can bind the textfield with a guard statement. Then we return the textfield value. Since our userText property is an optional, we can just return the text of the UITextField.

Map returns the Publisher so it fits right into the chaining of these calls. But unlike the sink that had a closure, we're only assigning the userText. The label won't be updated.

Assign returns a subscriber so we can't add a second assign call for the label. This brings up a great opportunity for another publisher example.

@PUBLISHED PROPERTY WRAPPER

We've already used the Published property wrapper in SwiftUI. However, that's part of the Combine framework so we can use it here.

This property wrapper adds a publisher to any property! So we're going to create a second publisher and a second subscriber.

1. Add the published property wrapper to the userText property. Also, give it a default value so it's not nil.

   ```
   @Published var userText : String? = ""
   ```

2. Add another subscriber property as an AnyCancellable Optional.

   ```
   var subscriber2 : AnyCancellable?
   ```

   Now we need to use that publisher and subscribe to it. We'll use the assign again. It will create the subscriber that assigns the value in our userText property to the label.

3. Create the publisher and subscriber in viewDidLoad.

   ```
   subscriber2 = $userText
       .assign(to: \.text, on: lbl)
   ```

That's it! The $ gives us access to the wrapped publisher. Then we create the subscriber with .assign specifying the key path and object.

In this case, the published value is a String Optional which is what the text property on a Label already is.

The functionality is back to what it was when we used the sink. Depending on the code, one route might make more sense than another.

223

Chapter Summary

We introduced some heavy concepts here with the Combine framework. Publishers publish updated values. Subscribers receive updated values. Again, going back to the Apple description of Combine, we are "processing values over time."

Publishers have outputs, and subscribers have inputs. The types of these must match. They also define Failure types which also must match. We implemented a Subscriber in our ViewController and made the types match. But we also learned about sink and assign which automatically match the types in their created subscribers.

You want to keep a reference to the subscriber created as an AnyCancellable. That allows you to cancel the subscription when needed. But also it prevents you from having to clean up the subscription manually. AnyCancellable does that for you in its deinit.

We also saw that Publishers support a variety of operators like map, reduce, and more. They return the same publisher so they can be chained before the subscriber is created. Operators are particularly helpful when you need to massage the updated value into something you need specifically.

The @Published property wrapper adds a publisher to any property. To access it, use the $ before the property and continue. You can add operators and subscribe to them like any other publisher.

These concepts already helped us in our SwiftUI work. But hopefully you agree that using these concepts can be useful in any project.

CHAPTER 16

URLSession Publisher

While this isn't a book on Combine, I do want to go through a few more things from the framework. Hopefully, this chapter will give you an idea of how to approach using Combine. Also, I hope that you'll see a more direct path for learning more in using this powerful framework.

In this chapter, we'll look at fetching data. We'll use a publisher and subscriber for that. We'll fetch data from a server which will lead to updating the UI. For testing/preview, we'll alternatively load data from a file also.

URLSession Publisher

If you've used URLSession before, you're familiar with creating a data task. URLSession also provides a data task publisher. It takes a URL as the parameter. It returns the publisher.

We've already seen how this works with the NotificationCenter and published wrapped properties. The concept isn't new in that sense, but we're now dealing with data returned. In our case, it will be data representing JSON.

When decoding JSON, errors can occur so we'll have to handle that as well.

© Bear Cahill 2021
B. Cahill, *UI Design for iOS App Development*,
https://doi.org/10.1007/978-1-4842-6449-2_16

I have provided a Ch16_BOC_StatusTracker.zip project for a starting point for this chapter. Let's look at the code.

Status Tracker Project

We're going to be loading user status data in JSON. There are three fields in the JSON: id, username, and status. Status can be one of three values: offline, paused, and live.

We want to be able to display the items in a list. We also want to be able to filter by the status value. The UI will look like Figure 16-1.

Figure 16-1. *Status Tracker App UI Design*

The usernames will be listed along with their associated status. The status options are listed at the top in a Picker (similar to a UIKit Segmented Control).

For the status value, we have an enumeration. The model for the data is a UserStatus struct. Both of these conform to Codable as you can see in Figure 16-2.

```swift
import Foundation
import Combine

enum Status : Int, Codable, CaseIterable {
    case offline, paused, live, all

    static var totalNum : Int {
        return Status.allCases.count
    }

    var description : String {
        switch self {
        case .offline:
            return "Offline"
        case .paused:
            return "Paused"
        case .live:
            return "Live"
        case .all:
            return "All"
        }
    }
}

struct UserStatus : Codable {
    var id = 0
    var username = ""
    var status = Status.offline
}
```

Figure 16-2. *Model Code*

Notice that at the top, we import Combine. That isn't used yet, but we know we're heading that way.

The underlying type for the Status is an Int. This can help in a few ways. We can create the Status value based on the selected index of the Picker. Also, we can store ints in our JSON instead of passing strings.

Status also conforms to Codable and CaseIterable. CaseIterable allows us to access the allCases array of the values. Accessing allCases helps iterating over the values or getting the total. I created a totalNum computed property to know how many values we have.

Notice there is an "all" value in the enum. This should only be used for the filtering.

The description property converts the values to a String.

This is just one option for implementing the Status enum. I find it to be clear, useful, and maintainable.

The UserStatus struct has the three values matching the keys in JSON that you can see in Figure 16-3.

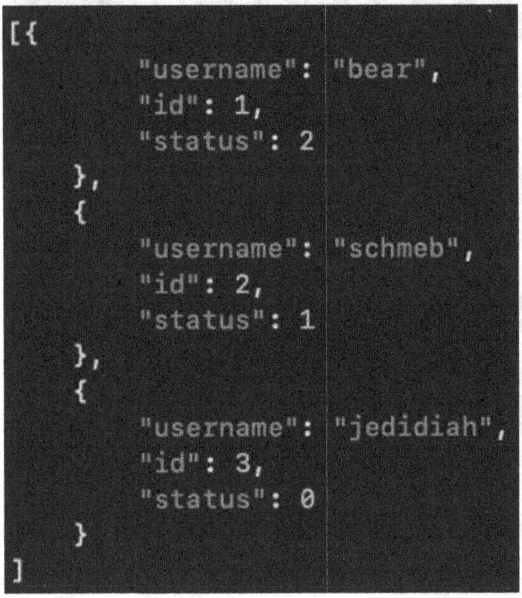

```
[{
        "username": "bear",
        "id": 1,
        "status": 2
    },
    {
        "username": "schmeb",
        "id": 2,
        "status": 1
    },
    {
        "username": "jedidiah",
        "id": 3,
        "status": 0
    }
]
```

Figure 16-3. *JSON Data*

A similar file is included in the project for test data. We'll load it from there but also from the server.

Status Tracker UI

The UI for the status tracker uses some elements we're familiar with and a new one: Picker. The elements are in a VStack with a Text element first.

The second element in the VStack is the Picker. The Picker takes a StringProtocol, a selection item to store the selection, and the items for selection.

We also need to specify a style for the picker. Without setting the style, it defaults to WheelPickerStyle which is like a Picker View in UIKit. We want a segmented picker style.

Finally, we have our list. It will loop over the status items with a .filter to find only the items we're interested in based on the selection in the Picker. Then it creates an HStack and two text items for each status array element. The ContentView code is in Figure 16-4.

```swift
struct ContentView: View {
    var mgr = UserStatusMgr.instance
    @State private var filterIndex : Int = Status.all.rawValue
    private var filterStatus : Status {
        Status(rawValue: self.filterIndex)!
    }

    var body: some View {
        VStack {
            Text("Status App")
                .fontWeight(.heavy)
            Picker("", selection: $filterIndex) {
                ForEach(0..<Status.totalNum) { (index) in
                    Text(Status(rawValue: index)!.description)
                }
            }.pickerStyle(SegmentedPickerStyle())

            List {
                ForEach(mgr.userStatus.filter
                { $0.status == self.filterStatus
                    || self.filterStatus == .all
                }, id: \.id) { item in
                    HStack {
                        Text(item.username)
                        Spacer()
                        Text(item.status.description)
                    }
                }
            }
        }
    }
}

struct ContentView_Previews: PreviewProvider {
    static var previews: some View {
        ContentView()
    }
}
```

Figure 16-4. *ContentView Code*

Notice that the filterIndex has a @State property wrapper, and the Picker uses this binding. When the user changes the Picker selection, this Int will be updated.

The filterStatus property is a computed property based on the user's filter selection. It's mostly just for easy checking in the .filter call for the list of users.

The preview code is unchanged from the generated code.

Model Manager

The first property in our ContentView is a UserStatusMgr instance. It uses a singleton defined in that class. The only place it's used is in the ForEach for our List item.

If we just looped over the mgr.userStatus property, it would list all the items. But we want to match the user's selected filter. We loop through the items in a .filter and include them if the status matches or if the user selected "All" in the picker.

The current UserStatusMgr code is just a couple of properties.

```
class UserStatusMgr {
    static let instance = UserStatusMgr()
    var userStatus = [UserStatus]()
}
```

It has the singleton property and the array for UserStatus items. We need to add the code to load the data from the server.

FETCHING DATA WITH A PUBLISHER

We want to publish the userStatus property for updating the UI. So we have to add the ObservableObject protocol to the class and mark the property with @Published. Then we can set the class to be an ObservedObject in our UI.

We also need to fetch the data from the server. Then we can parse it and update the userStatus property to get published.

1. Declare the UserStatusMgr class as conforming to the ObservableObject protocol.

    ```
    class UserStatusMgr : ObservableObject {
    ```

2. Add the @Published wrapper to the userStatus property.

    ```
    @Published var userStatus = [UserStatus]()
    ```

3. Create a private init for the singleton that calls the update function for the status data (to be written next).

    ```
    private init() {
        updateStatusData()
    }
    ```

4. Create a function named updateStatus data that creates the URL instance.

    ```
    func updateStatusData() {
        guard let url =
        URL(string:
              "https://brainwashinc.com/Status.json")
              else { return }
    }
    ```

5. After the guard in the preceding updateStatusData function, create the URLSession publisher.

    ```
    URLSession.shared
        .dataTaskPublisher(for: url)
    ```

The publisher for a URLSession data task publisher defines its output and failure. The output is a tuple of Data and URLResponse. The names are data and response, respectively. The failure is a URLError.

In this case, we just want to get the data, but that's just part of the tuple. We can use .map to massage the data a bit.

6. Add .map to the publisher to convert the response tuple to just the data item.

```
URLSession.shared
    .dataTaskPublisher(for: url)
    .map { $0.data }
```

The result of the map is a publisher that just passes the Data item downstream. We want to decode that Data since it's JSON. Since this is such a common action, Combine provides a .decode operator.

7. Add the .decode operator after .map.

```
URLSession.shared
    .dataTaskPublisher(for: url)
    .map { $0.data }
    .decode(type: [UserStatus].self,
        decoder: JSONDecoder())
```

The decode returns a publisher that passes a Decodable downstream, which is great. But it also has a Failure of Error. Since JSON parsing may not work, we have to deal with this case.

There are various ways to handle this. We'll look at a simple one here. Using .sink is another useful option I encourage you to look into.

8. Add the .replaceError after the decode.

```
URLSession.shared
    .dataTaskPublisher(for: url)
    .map { $0.data }
    .decode(type: [UserStatus].self,
        decoder: JSONDecoder())
    .replaceError(with: self.userStatus)
```

Now if the JSONDecoder has an error, we just continue on with the current value of self.userStatus. This still returns a publisher so we need to move on to the subscriber.

9. Add .receive to publish on the main thread.

```
URLSession.shared
    .dataTaskPublisher(for: url)
    .map { $0.data }
    .decode(type: [UserStatus].self,
        decoder: JSONDecoder())
    .replaceError(with: self.userStatus)
    .receive(on: DispatchQueue.main)
```

Now we're at the end of the publisher chain and need to create the subscription.

10. Create an AnyCancellable named subscriber as a property of the UserStatusMgr class.

```
var subscriber : AnyCancellable?
```

11. Add an .assign modifier to assign the value and store the result in the property from step 10.

```
subscriber = URLSession.shared
    .dataTaskPublisher(for: url)
    .map { $0.data }
    .decode(type: [UserStatus].self,
```

```
        decoder: JSONDecoder())
    .replaceError(with: self.userStatus)
    .receive(on: DispatchQueue.main)
    .assign(to: \.userStatus, on: self)
```

Running the app at this point works, but it doesn't load the data into the UI. That's because we create the UI with the UserStatusMgr's initial values of userStatus which is blank.

We need to mark the ContentView's mgr property as an Observed Object. Then we'll get updates when the userStatus property is published. That will cause the UI to be updated.

12.   Add @ObservedObject to the mgr property in ContentView.

```
struct ContentView: View {
    @ObservedObject var mgr = UserStatusMgr.instance
```

Now the app shows the UI and also gets updated once the data is fetched. Using the filter works also as in Figure 16-5.

Figure 16-5. *App Running with Filtered List*

This publisher only runs once. The task runs and publishes and stops. If you run updateStatusData again, it will fetch new data and continue.

Not only did we see how to fetch data with a publisher but also some other operators. I encourage you to research the operators in Combine on your own to see all that is available.

Debug Data

For development and testing, we may not want to hit the server every time. Instead we can include code to read a test file from our project bundle.

One option is to just load the file data and parse it into the userStatus property. That would work fine.

Here's one solution that loads the data in the background for debug builds and publishes on the UI thread. If this code is at the top of updateStatusData, it will run for debug builds.

Note   We'll add a variation of this code to the project later. There's no need to add it now unless you want to experiment.

```
#if DEBUG
guard let urlLocal = Bundle.main.url(
                        forResource: "Status",
                        withExtension: "json")
    else { return }
DispatchQueue.global().async {
    if let data = try? Data(contentsOf: urlLocal) {
        DispatchQueue.main.async {
            self.userStatus = (try? JSONDecoder()
                .decode([UserStatus].self,
                        from: data))
```

```
            ?? self.userStatus
        }
    }
}
return
#endif
```

This code creates the bundle URL, reads the data (background), and decodes the JSON. When the userStatus is updated, it will get published. It's fine, but it's a bit redundant and doesn't exercise our existing code when testing.

We can come up with a more interesting solution using another subscription.

For one thing, it will give us a chance to work through some more publisher-subscriber examples. Also, we will likely be able to reuse code, and that will exercise more of our production code in testing.

Let's set the loaded data (server or local) in a property and create a subscriber to that property. In the new subscriber, we can process the JSON data and update the userStatus property.

USING LOCAL TEST DATA

We need a new property to store the Data instance. Also, we need another subscriber property. We can update the updateStatusData to use the local file route for debug builds to avoid server hits.

1. In UserStatusMgr, create two new properties statusData (of type Data and initialized) and subscriberData (of type AnyCancellable Optional).

   ```
   @Published var statusData = Data()
   var subscriberData : AnyCancellable?
   ```

We will store the JSON data in statusData. Since it's published, we can create a subscription to it. Then, whenever it's updated, we'll process the new data.

2. Create a new function in UserStatusMgr to create the publisher-subscriber.

```
func createSubscription() {
    $statusData
}
```

I wrote earlier that there are other ways to handle the error from the decode. One way is with a .catch operator. The problem here is if it does catch an error, it will cancel the subscription by replacing the publisher with a new one. In our case, that might be OK since our publisher should only execute the task once.

However, if we want to support ongoing publishing, we don't want this cancelled. Instead we can use .flatMap. The .flatMap call takes the input from the upstream and returns a publisher. In there we can do the decode. If it fails, we can catch it.

We'll use .flatMap here to see how it works.

3. Add .flatMap to the publisher.

```
func createSubscription() {
    $statusData
        .flatMap{ data in return Just(data)
            }
}
```

At this point, flatMap just takes the data and creates a new publisher with Just. Just simply publishes the data and ends.

We're going to add operators to the Just that will decode the JSON and catch the error. If there's an error, we can use another Just to publish the current value of userStatus.

4. Add the call for decoding the JSON and catching the possible error.

```
func createSubscription() {
    $statusData
        .flatMap{ data in
            return Just(data)
                .decode(type: [UserStatus].self,
                    decoder: JSONDecoder())
            .catch { _ in
                return Just(self.userStatus)
            }
        }
}
```

Now we have the publisher we want. We get the publisher of the statusData property and create a publisher with .flatMap. That takes the data and creates another publisher with Just. Operators on that publisher decode the JSON.

If there's an error decoding the data, we publish the current self.userStatus. The catch will replace the current publisher (the first Just) with another Just.

5. Add .receive to create the final version of our publisher.

```
createSubscription() {
    $statusData
        .flatMap{ data in
            return Just(data)
                .decode(type: [UserStatus].self,
                    decoder: JSONDecoder())
```

```
        .catch { _ in
            return Just(self.userStatus)
        }
    }
    .receive(on: DispatchQueue.main)
}
```

6. Add .assign to create the subscription. Store the subscription in
    the new AnyCancellable property created in step 1.

```
createSubscription() {
    subscriberData =
        $statusData
            .flatMap{ data in
                return Just(data)
                    .decode(type: [UserStatus].self,
                        decoder: JSONDecoder())
                .catch { _ in
                    return Just(self.userStatus)
                }
        }
        .receive(on: DispatchQueue.main)
        .assign(to: \.userStatus, on: self)
}
```

On our resulting publisher from .assign, we created our subscription.
Now once the data is processed, we save the userStatus array. This is
a published property, and the UI will get updated.

Back in our updateStatusData function, we no longer want to set
userStatus. Instead we want to set statusData with just the Data value.
Then the subscription to statusData we created will process it, and
userStatus will be published.

The subscription in updateUserStatus just needs to receive the data, map it, handle the error, and assign to the property. Also, since we're not causing the publication to the UI data, we no longer need the .receive modifier.

7.   Update the updateStatusData function to remove the JSON parsing and .receive modifier. The .assign needs to set statusData (instead of userStatus) since we're dealing with the data now. The updated code looks like Figure 16-6.

```
func updateStatusData() {
    guard let url = URL(string:
                "https://brainwashinc.com/Status.json")
                else { return }

    subscriber = URLSession.shared
                .dataTaskPublisher(for: url)
                .map { $0.data }
                .replaceError(with: self.statusData)
                .assign(to: \.statusData, on: self)
}
```

Figure 16-6.   *Current updateStatusData Function*

We need to make sure the function to create the subscription is called.

8.   Add a call to createSubscription in init.

```
private init() {
    createSubscription()
    updateStatusData()
}
```

If you run the app now, it should work as it did before but with two subscriptions. Our original subscriber in updateStatusData still receives the server data. However, now it just stores it in the statusData property.

The new subscriber in createSubscription receives that Data instance and parses it. The parsed data is now stored in our userStatus array which gets published on the main thread.

The steps in this exercise up to this point split out the loading of the data into two parts. The first gets the data. The second parses it.

Now we can add the option to load the data locally. This replaces the server hit of the first part when building for debugging. The second part will still operate the same. When the data is stored, the subscription on it will parse and set it in the array.

9. In updateStatusData, add test code at the top of the function to load the JSON data from a file within a DEBUG conditional.

```
func updateStatusData() {
    #if DEBUG
    guard let urlLocal = Bundle.main.url(
                        forResource: "Status",
                        withExtension: "json")
        else { return }

        if let data = try? Data(contentsOf: urlLocal) {
            DispatchQueue.global().async {
                self.statusData = data
        }
    }
    return
    #endif
    ...
```

For production builds, we have a subscription that receives the data. For debug, we just load the data locally. Whether we get the data from the server or a local file, the parsing is done via a subscription to the data property.

Note   To avoid the compiler warning, you can remove the return in the preceding code, change the #endif to a #else, and put #endif at the end of the function. See the EOC code for this chapter for details.

If you run the app now, the data should be loaded from the file and the UI updated. The local data has "-test" appended to the usernames to tell which data is loaded as in Figure 16-7.

Figure 16-7. *UI with Local Test Data*

Production builds will disregard the DEBUG conditional and load data from the server.

Chapter Summary

We went through a lot of variations in this chapter's code. We saw how to create a publisher from a URLSession. The resulting data task publisher can be modified with operators like other publishers. We can map the data, decode, replace errors, assign, and more.

242

We also created a variation for local test data. This route used flatMap to decode the data and catch any errors. It uses Just in a couple of places and also avoided a cancelled subscription if an error occurred.

In the end, we had two published properties and two subscribers.

Our ContentView declared the UserStatusMgr property as an observed object. This is for when the updates occur, our UI will reflect the changes.

The second subscriber was on the statusData property. Whether it's changed via the local data loading or the server returned data, our second subscriber takes care of it. Now we have one place where the data is parsed, set on userStatus, and published for the UI.

As I hope you see, there are various ways of accomplishing what you need to do. It will depend on your specific needs as to which solution is best. My intention is to show you a variety of ways. But, again, this isn't a book on Combine.

We looked at only a portion of the list of operators. With further study, some will be familiar like map, filter, reduce, compactMap, count, max, contains, drop, and so on. Some will be related to those with the prefix "try" such as tryMap, tryFilter, tryReduce, and more.

Some operators may be new to you like sink, zip, combineLatest, and merge. I hope you check them all out!

CHAPTER 17

Transitions and Animation

Often, when I'm teaching iOS development in person, we discuss various ways to animate the UI. There are plenty of ways and options in animation. However, most of the time, we really aren't trying to do something too complex.

I primarily develop for clients who need something for their business. It might be a customer-facing app, a companion to their website, or an app for viewing data.

Typically, there is very little room for animation. I might fade something in/out for displaying. Sometimes, I have a menu or similar that needs to move. But spectacular animation usually doesn't factor in.

I say all of this because while I want to show you how to animate in SwiftUI, the focus should be on the options. This chapter will hopefully give you the tools to know some of what's possible and how to find out more. Just don't think we're going to build a 3D game or anything like that.

Transitions

Transitions are what control how a visual element is inserted or removed from the view. The insertion and removal aren't automatically animated, but they can be.

© Bear Cahill 2021
B. Cahill, *UI Design for iOS App Development*,
https://doi.org/10.1007/978-1-4842-6449-2_17

There are built-in transitions that do a variety of presentations that are common. Some of these are opacity, move, scale, and slide. The move transition requires an Edge value. This lets it know where to start: top, bottom, leading, or trailing.

Let's add a few UI items to see a transition work.

TRANSITION ON TEXT

We're going to start with a new SwiftUI project. We're going to add a Button to toggle a value. Based on that value, we'll add a Text item to the UI. We'll then add a transition to that item for inserting and removing it.

1. Create a new SwiftUI project (I named mine VariousUI) with SwiftUI for the interface and SwiftUI App for the life cycle (see Figure 17-1).

Figure 17-1. *New Project Options*

2. Add a toggle property to the ContentView in ContentView.swift.

```
@State var isToggled = false
```

3. In the body computed property of ContentView, replace the
    default content with a VStack.

```
var body: some View {
    VStack {
    }
}
```

4. In the VStack, create a Button to toggle the value.

```
Button(action: {
    self.isToggled.toggle()
}) {
    Text("Toggle")
}
```

5. We'll add another Text item, below the button, for
    "Toggled" if the property is set to true.

```
if isToggled {
    Text("Toggled")
}
```

Running the app now shows a "Toggle" button. If you tap the button, a
Textfield is displayed like Figure 17-2.

Figure 17-2. Toggle Button and Text

Next, we'll add a transition to have the Text appear in a different way.

247

6. Add a transition to the Text item.

```
Text("Toggled")
    .transition(.move(edge: .top))
```

If you run the app now, you will still see the Text pop on and off the screen. We need to add some animation.

7. Add animation to the Text item.

```
Text("Toggled")
    .transition(.move(edge: .top))
    .animation(.easeInOut)
```

Animation has a variety of options as you can see in Figure 17-3.

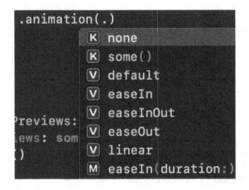

Figure 17-3. *Partial List of Animations*

Feel free to try different types of animations. I like spring a lot.

Now when you run the app (or Live mode preview), you should see the Text item move from the top when added. It should also move to the top when removed.

Asymmetric Transitions

Often we want to transition something on the screen one way but off the screen a different way. For that, we create an asymmetric transition. The function to create one takes two parameters: insertion and removal. There are just two transitions.

So if we want to insert a UI element with opacity but use a scale to remove it, that's not a problem.

ASYMMETRIC TRANSITION

Let's create an asymmetric transition for our Text item. If you experimented with the different transitions already, you've seen opacity and scale. We'll use those.

1. Replace the transition used before (i.e., move(edge: .top)) with a call to .asymmetric.

```
Text("Toggled")
    .transition(
        .asymmetric(
```

2. For insertion, we'll use opacity. For removal, pass in a slide.

```
Text("Toggled")
    .transition(
        .asymmetric(
            insertion: .opacity,
            removal: .slide))
```

Run the app. What happened? It's not animated anymore! Transitions don't animate in implicit animations like this. We need to use an explicit animation.

3. Add an implicit animation using withAnimation around the
    toggle value change in the Button action.

```
Button(action: {
    withAnimation(.easeInOut(duration: 1)) {
        self.isToggled.toggle()
    }
}
```

One second is being passed in as the duration. Feel free to pass
in whatever duration you like (or none as we did before).

Now the transition should work and animate. But what if we
want it to fade in and move or some other transition? We can
combine them.

4. Call combine on the opacity transition and pass in a move.

```
Text("Toggled")
    .transition(
        .asymmetric(
            insertion: AnyTransition
                .opacity
                .combined(with:
                    .move(edge: .top)),
            removal: .slide))
```

Now that we have it working the way we'd like, let's clean it up.
We'll create a separate transition for what we've created. We
can do that as an extension of the AnyTransition struct.

5. Create an extension of AnyTransition (it's fine to have it in the
    same file).

```
extension AnyTransition {
}
```

6. Declare a static var named textTransition of type AnyTransition.

```
static var textTransition : AnyTransition
```

7. Implement the get (no keyword needed) of the textTransition to create the transition we created in our code.

```
static var textTransition : AnyTransition {
    AnyTransition
        .asymmetric(
            insertion: AnyTransition
                .opacity
                .combined(with:
                    .move(edge: .top)),
            removal: .slide)
}
```

8. Now use the newly defined transition instead of the several lines of code we moved to textTransition.

```
Text("Toggled")
    .transition(.textTransition)
```

Run the code and verify the transition is the same as before.

In this exercise, not only did we combine transitions, we also created a custom one to use in other places.

Animations

We've already seen a little about animating a transition. There's a few other things we want to look at animating.

Various modifier changes can be animated. Some common ones might be size/scale, color, shadow, rotation, and blur.

Animations on modifiers can be done with implicit or explicit animations. Also, you can set different implicit animation modifiers on different changes.

ANIMATING CHANGES

In this exercise, we'll look at animating various changes to UI elements.

1. At the bottom of the VStack, add a circle to the UI.

   ```
   Circle()
   ```

2. Make the color of the circle red.

   ```
   Circle()
       .foregroundColor(.red)
   ```

   In the preview, you should see a big red circle in the UI as in Figure 17-4.

Figure 17-4. *Circle Added to the UI*

3. Add shadow, scaleEffect, and blur modifiers to the circle all
    based on the isToggle value.

```
Circle()
    .foregroundColor(.red)
        .shadow(radius: isToggled ? 10 : 50)
        .scaleEffect(isToggled ? 0.75 : 1)
        .blur(radius: isToggled ? 5 : 0)
```

Now when you run the app and toggle the value, you should see
a shadowed, smaller red circle that's blurred like Figure 17-5.

Figure 17-5. *Toggle Value True Affecting the UI*

This works fine and is animated. But it doesn't seem very lively for a
bright red ball. Let's add an animation modifier to give it some life.

4. After the scaleEffect modifier, add an animation modifier. Use
    spring and pass in a damping fraction of 0.5.

```
Circle()
    .foregroundColor(.red)
        .shadow(radius: isToggled ? 10 : 50)
        .scaleEffect(isToggled ? 0.5 : 1)
        .animation(.spring(dampingFraction : 0.5))
        .blur(radius: isToggled ? 5 : 0)
```

The damping fraction is the amount of drag applied to the value being animated. The default is 0.825 and doesn't provide as much bounce. Our 0.5 is pretty good. Setting it to something small like 0.15 makes it oscillate around the final value several times. Try it out.

Spring has other parameters you can pass in as well. I encourage you to check those out sometime.

As you run the app, you should notice that the animation for the shadow and scale use the spring animation. This also uses its only timing. The explicit withAnimation call is still one second and applied to the blur. If it's not noticeable, make the withAnimation duration five seconds and test it out.

ViewModifier Protocol

We have several modifiers on our red circle. If we like this combination, we might want to save it as something to use in other places in our code.

For our Transition, we did that as an extension of AnyTransition. Our static computed property was declared as a type of AnyTransition. For our modifiers, it will be a struct that conforms to the ViewModifier protocol.

The ViewModifier protocol is very similar to the View. However, the body is a function instead of a property. This body function takes a Content and returns a View. The Content is the value the modifier is used on. In our case, it's a type that implements View.

CREATE A VIEW MODIFIER

We are going to create a struct that implements ViewModifier. We have a required function of the body that takes a Content (in our case, a type that implements View) and returns a View.

1. Declare the struct (in the same file is fine).

    ```
    struct BouncyModifier : ViewModifier {
    }
    ```

2. Declare a property for the amount to blur the View.

    ```
    struct BouncyModifier : ViewModifier {
        var blurFactor : CGFloat
    }
    ```

3. Declare the body function.

    ```
    struct BouncyModifier : ViewModifier {
        var blurFactor : CGFloat
            func body(content: Content) -> some View {
        }
    }
    ```

4. Implement the body function to add the modifiers to the parameter passed in.

    ```
    return content
        .shadow(radius: blurFactor > 0 ? 10 : 50)
        .scaleEffect(blurFactor > 0 ? 0.5 : 1.0)
        .animation(
            .spring(dampingFraction : 0.15))
        .blur(radius: blurFactor)
    ```

5. Use the new modifier instead of the previous list of modifiers.

    ```
    Circle()
        .foregroundColor(.red)
        .modifier(BouncyModifier(blurFactor:
            isToggled ? 5 : 0))
    ```

    Run the app and notice that the animation is the same but with a little more spring.

There's another option rather than using the .modifier to create the ViewModifier. We can create an extension on View to do it for us.

In the end, it's the same thing, just in a different place. It can help keep the View code clean too.

6. Define an extension of View (in the same file is fine).

```
extension View {
}
```

7. Define a "bouncy" function that takes a CGFloat and returns a View.

```
extension View {
    func bouncy(blurFactor: CGFloat)
        -> some View {
    }
}
```

8. Return a modifier that creates a BouncyModifier created with the parameter passed in.

```
extension View {
    func bouncy(blurFactor: CGFloat)
        -> some View {
        self.modifier(
            BouncyModifier(blurFactor: blurFactor))
    }
}
```

9. Use this function on your Circle instead of the .modifier with BouncyModifier.

```
Circle()
    .foregroundColor(.red)
    .bouncy(blurFactor: isToggled ? 5 : 0)
```

> By creating a ViewModifier and extension on View, our code is cleaner. We can reuse either of these in other places in our project. Also, we can make changes in one place that affect our bouncy animation throughout our app.

As I mentioned, there are animation functions for affecting the performance of animations. Several of these are for the curve of the animation timing. These functions, easeIn, easeOut, easeInOut, and linear, have forms that take a Double for duration. The duration is the number of seconds for the animation.

The timingCurve function allows the developer to specify the timing curve as a Bézier path coordinate and a duration.

We've seen spring with its default values for response, dampingFraction and blendDuration. There's also interactiveSpring. It's basically the same but with different default values for interactive animations. The interpolatingSpring allows you to specify mass and stiffness (of the spring) along with damping and initial velocity.

Other functions are delay, speed, and two for repeating: repeatCount and repeatForever.

All of these functions allow you to customize your animations. Honestly, most of the time that I use animations, I can stick to a lot of defaults. Sometimes, I need a specific duration. In those cases, I usually use 0.37 which matches a lot of system animations such as displaying the keyboard. About the only other variation I use is spring to give some bounce.

Gradients

Let's add a little color to our circle. We can create a gradient to use in filling in our circle. An easy way to create a Gradient instance is by passing in some colors. The resulting Gradient will interpolate the variations in between.

To fill our circle, we'll use the .fill modifier. We pass in something that conforms to the ShapeStyle protocol. Color does that, and we can pass a color into .fill.

```
Circle().fill(Color.blue)
```

Other structs that implement ShapeStyle are ForegroundStyle, ImagePaint, LinearGradient, RadialGradient, and AngularGradient.

ADDING COLOR TO THE CIRCLE

We're going to create a gradient and fill in the circle. Now our animation will have more life given a bit of definition to our element.

1. Create a gradient as a property of the ContentView.

    ```
    struct ContentView: View {
        @State var isToggled = false
        let gradient = Gradient(colors:
            [.purple, .yellow,
            .green])
    ```

2. At the top of the body, above the VStack, add a RadialGradient.

    ```
    var body: some View {
        let radialGradient = RadialGradient(gradient:
                            gradient,
                            center: .center,
                            startRadius: 1.0,
                            endRadius: 250.0)
        VStack {...
    ```

3. Use the created radial gradient in the previous step in a .fill
    modifier of the Circle instead of the .foreground.

```
Circle()
    .fill(radialGradient)
    .bouncy(blurFactor: isToggled ? 5 : 0)
```

Run the app and see the colors as in Figure 17-6.

Figure 17-6. *Circle with Radial Gradient After the Animation*

4. Create an AngularGradient below the radialGradient
    from step 2.

```
let angularGradient = AngularGradient(gradient:
            gradient,
            center: .center,
            angle: .degrees(0))
```

5. Use this new angularGradient in the .fill.

```
Circle()
    .fill(angularGradient)
```

Run the app and see the new color fill as in Figure 17-7.

Figure 17-7. *Circle with Radial Gradient After the Animation*

Now we have more color in our circle to give it even more life.

Rotation

Rotating UI elements is another common alteration. It's also a good change for animation. There are two modifiers we can use to rotate our circle easily.

The rotationEffect modifier takes two parameters. The first parameter is the angle of rotation. The second parameter is an optional point around which to rotate. The default point is the center.

```
.rotationEffect(.degrees(90))
```

NOTE   We'll add these rotation effects to the code in the next exercise.

The rotation3DEffect also takes the angle of rotation and the axis of rotation. The anchor (default to center), anchorZ (default to 0), and perspective (default to 1) have defaults so they're not required.

The axis specifies one or more axes to rotate around. If we only specify the Z axis, it will behave just like the .rotationEffect.

```
.rotation3DEffect(Angle(degrees: 90),
                  axis: (x: 0, y: 0, z: 1))
```

The Z axis goes front and back. The X axis goes left and right. The Y axis goes up and down.

Let's try some.

ADDING ROTATION

We'll start with adding rotation to spin our circle. Then we'll add 3D rotation and see some real action.

1. Add .rotationEffect after our custom .bouncy modifier.

    Base the rotation on the isToggled property.

    ```
    Circle()
        .fill(angularGradient)
        .bouncy(blurFactor: isToggled ? 5 : 0)
        .rotationEffect(.degrees(isToggled ? 90 : 0))
    ```

    Run the app and see that the circle rotated like Figure 17-8.

Figure 17-8. *Circle After the Animation*

261

2. Remove the .rotationEffect and use the .rotation3DEffect instead but only for the Z axis.

```
.rotation3DEffect(Angle(degrees: isToggled ? 90 : 0),
                  axis: (x: 0, y: 0, z: 1))
```

Run the app and the result should look the same as Figure 17-7.

3. Change the axis to the X axis (zeroes for the other two).

```
.rotation3DEffect(Angle(degrees: isToggled ? 90 : 0),
                  axis: (x: 1, y: 0, z: 0))
```

If you run the app, you'll see the animation partially flips the circle to be flat and not visible.

Using the Y axis does the same except it flips it in the other direction.

4. Use all three axes in the rotation call and change the angle to 300.

```
.rotation3DEffect(Angle(degrees:
                   isToggled ? 300 : 0),
                   axis: (x: 1, y: 1, z: 1))
```

Running the code now shows a bit more action. It's a bit fast so let's slow it down.

5. Add an animation after the .rotation3DEffect with spring and a speed setting.

```
.animation(.spring().speed(0.1))
```

If you get an error, it's because the compiler can't determine the context. Add "Animation" before .spring to help out.

```
.animation(Animation.spring().speed(0.1))
```

Speed takes a multiplier for the animation time. Using 0.10 causes the animation to take 10% of whatever speed is related to the animation. The default animation is 0.37 so our rotation should take about 4 seconds.

The end result should look like Figure 17-9.

Figure 17-9. *Circle After a 3D Rotation*

We now have three animations in our app. The first is an implicit animation in the Button action to animate the change in the toggle property. This animates the Text for the "Toggled" element.

Another animation handles the BouncyModifier. It uses .spring with a parameter for the damping fraction.

The third animation is on our rotation 3D effect where we use .spring and .speed.

Let's make one more change to the animation of the rotation.

6. Change the .spring and .speed calls to a .linear with a duration
    of 0.75 seconds.

```
Circle()
    .fill(angularGradient)
    .bouncy(blurFactor: isToggled ? 5 : 0)
    .rotation3DEffect(Angle(degrees:
                      isToggled ? 300 : 0),
                      axis: (x: 1, y: 1, z: 1))
    .animation(.linear(duration: 0.75))
```

The appearance at the end of the animation is the same as before. However,
the animation is a set time (not relative with a multiplier). You may notice the
start and stop of the rotation are a bit static. Linear doesn't speed up and slow
down during the animation curve.

DrawingGroup

Our circle is drawing and animating very well. However, if we're trying
to do a large number of animations at the same time, it may take a
performance hit.

Let's say we put 100 of our circles on the screen. That's a lot of
animation: rotation, shadow, scale, and blur.

Using a drawing group can help with performance here. If we put all
of the circles in a drawing group, it will render the View offscreen first and
then put it on the screen. This is a faster method of rendering.

Also, drawing groups use the Metal framework in the background. This
works more directly with the GPU for faster graphic processing.

USING METAL IN SWIFT

In this exercise, we'll add 100 circles to our UI. We'll do this in two stacks, but otherwise the code will stay the same. The performance will take a big hit during the animation. We'll solve this by using a drawing group.

1. Replace your single circle with 100 circles. To do this, use a VStack with a ForEach with a range of zero to nine. Inside the VStack, create an HStack with another zero to nine ForEach. Inside that nested ForEach, create the circle.

```
VStack {
    ForEach(0..<10, id: \.self) { index in
        HStack {
            ForEach(0..<10, id: \.self) { index2 in
                Circle()
                    .fill(angularGradient)
                    .bouncy(blurFactor:
                        self.isToggled ? 5 : 0)
                    .rotation3DEffect(Angle(degrees:
                        self.isToggled ? 300 : 0),
                        axis: (x: 1, y: 1, z: 1))
                    .animation(.linear(duration:
                        0.75))
            }
        }
    }
}
```

Run the app and verify 100 circles are added to the UI as in Figure 17-10. You'll notice the circles are much smaller. However, our shadow setting is still quite high. This causes the shadows to blend together and cover much of the screen.

265

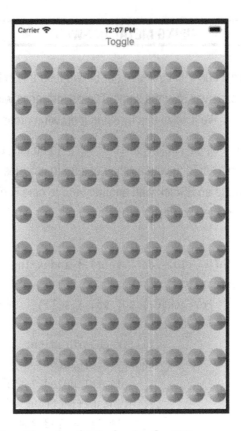

Figure 17-10. *One Hundred Circles in the UI*

If you tap the Toggle button, notice the jittery animation.

2. Add .drawingGroup to the outer VStack (created in step 1) of the circles that you added in step 1.

```
...}.drawingGroup()
```

Run the app again and notice how much smoother it animates.

Chapter Summary

In this chapter, we looked at a lot of UI aspects. We started by learning about Transitions for adding/removing items to/from the UI. For animating transitions, we looked at various types of Transitions and the .animation modifier.

To combine animations, we used asymmetric transitions with the .combine function on a Transition. Once our transition was the way we wanted it, we moved it into a static computed property in an extension on AnyTransition.

We expanded our UI with a Circle and learned some new modifiers for scaling, shadows, and blurring. Animating those based on the toggle value was done via the .animation call.

Our combination of modifiers was moved to a ViewModifier struct called BouncyModifier. We also defined a function in an extension of View to create the BouncyModifier. That modifier was added to our Circle instead of all the code right in place.

Using the ViewModifier also makes the effects reusable in other places in our code.

Defining and using gradients gave our circle more definition. And adding animation gave it more life. We explored various options for animation including the curve, timing, spring, and axes in 3D space.

We improved the performance for the 100 circles with a drawing group that uses the Metal framework.

Putting this all together shows the various approaches to animation and changes you can make to UI elements. These same types of modifiers and animation can be applied to a Text, Button, or other visual elements.

CHAPTER 18

App Including WatchKit

In this chapter, we're going to build a small but functional app. We want to go through this exercise so we know we can do it end to end.

We're going to build a tip calculator. It's my "go-to" project most of the time – partially because the requirements are basically built into the name.

It's a good exercise for having to get user input, manipulate it in some way (functionality), and update the UI. Of course, the input data we need are the bill amount and tip percentage.

There are many ways we can get this information from the user: textfields, pickers, sliders, and more. We'll use a TextField for the bill amount and a Picker for the tip percentage.

The functionality will be simple. In fact, we won't even need a function or closure in the normal sense. We can use computed properties instead.

We want the UI to look like Figure 18-1.

© Bear Cahill 2021
B. Cahill, *UI Design for iOS App Development*,
https://doi.org/10.1007/978-1-4842-6449-2_18

Figure 18-1. Tip Calculator UI

Feel free to try to write the app now without looking further. Or read the next sections on properties and UI design and then try it. See if you can apply the binding, UI elements, and other things you've learned.

Properties

As I mentioned earlier, we need two pieces of input: bill amount and tip percentage. These will be our properties wrapped in @State property wrappers and updated as the input changes.

We'll also have a property for the array of tip percentages for the user to choose from.

Displaying the values to the users means we have to calculate the values. This can be done in computed properties. We need at least two: tip amount and total.

Also, the output should be displayed as formatted for currency. The NumberFormatter class works well for this. We can have another computed property to create and configure a NumberFormatter.

UI Design

We can use Text items for the title and two output areas. That only leaves the input. We can use a TextField and Picker as mentioned before. These each use binding to the related properties.

In many places, we'll add some spacing, padding, font weight, and so on to make the UI look good.

TIP CALCULATOR

First, we need to create a new project. We'll add our properties to the ContentView next. Finally, we'll create the body computed property contents.

1. Create a new project called TC using the watchOS template for "iOS App with Watch App" as in Figure 18-2. Use SwiftUI for the interface and SwiftUI App for the life cycle.

Figure 18-2. *iOS App with Watch App Template*

2. Add the two properties to be the source of truth for the user's input.

```
struct ContentView: View {
    @State private var tipSelected = 1
    @State private var billInput = ""
```

271

3. Add the tip percentages for the user selected.

```
private var tipPercentages = [0.1, 0.15,
            0.2, 0.25]
```

4. Add a computed property for the number formatter.

```
private var numFormatter : NumberFormatter {
    let nf = NumberFormatter()
    nf.numberStyle = .currency
    nf.isLenient = true
    return nf
}
```

5. Create a computed property for the billAmount (double of the entered bill amount).

```
private var billAmount : Double {
    numFormatter.number(from:
        billInput)?
        .doubleValue ?? 0.0
}
```

6. Create a computed property for the tip amount using the billAmount defined in step 5.

```
private var tipAmount : Double {
    billAmount * tipPercentages[tipSelected] }
```

7. Create a computed property for the total using the billAmount from step 5 and tipAmount from step 6.

```
private var total : Double { tipAmount + billAmount }
```

8. Replace the default body contents with a VStack and the app title including padding at the end.

```
var body: some View {
    VStack {
        Text("Tip Calculator")
            .fontWeight(.heavy)
    }.padding()
```

9. Add a TextField with binding to the billInput property.

```
TextField("Bill Amount", text: $billInput)
    .textFieldStyle(RoundedBorderTextFieldStyle())
```

10. Create a Picker with binding to the tipSelected property based on the tip percentages array in a ForEach.

```
Picker("Tip", selection: $tipSelected) {
    ForEach (tipPercentages.indices, id: \.self) {
        let dbl = Double(self.tipPercentages[$0])
        Text("\(Int(dbl * 100.0))%")
    }
}

.pickerStyle(SegmentedPickerStyle())
```

11. Add an HStack with the Text items for output using the number formatter.

```
HStack {
    let tipStr = numFormatter.string(for: tipAmount)
    Text("Tip: \(tipStr ?? "$0.00")")
    Spacer()

    let totalStr = numFormatter.string(for: total)
    Text("Total: \(totalStr ?? "$0.00")")
}

Spacer()
```

The preview should look like Figure 18-1. If we run the app and enter 20 for the bill amount, we should see the tip and total displayed as in Figure 18-3.

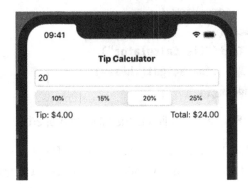

Figure 18-3. *Tip Calculator with Tip and Total*

There were some spacers and such added in there for the UI. Overall, it's a simple app with a simple UI, but it works. I hope each step felt familiar and comfortable.

WatchKit

Now we want to take this UI and use it in the Watch app module. For the most part, the UI will work as it does for iOS.

Many UI items in SwiftUI work across platforms. However, in some cases, variations don't exist. For us, that will be limited to the TextField and Picker.

WATCH APP

You'll notice in the current project that there is already a "TC WatchKit App" and a "TC WatchKit Extension." We'll be editing the ContentView.swift file in the extension.

1. Open the ContentView.swift file in the TC iOS app (**not the extension**).

2. Copy the entire contents of the file.

3. Open the ContentView.swift file in the TC WatchKit Extension.

4. Paste the copied code over the entire file.

    There will be two errors. Both of them are for styles – the TextField and Picker.

5. Comment out the code for the styles.

    ```
    //.textFieldStyle(RoundedBorderTextFieldStyle())

        ...

        //.pickerStyle(SegmentedPickerStyle())
    ```

6. Refresh the preview, and the Canvas should display a watch preview like Figure 18-4.

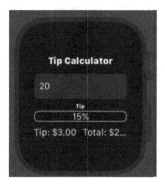

Figure 18-4. *WatchKit App Preview*

275

If you run the app in Live mode, be sure to first pick the appropriate target and simulator in Xcode (top left) as in Figure 18-5.

Figure 18-5. *Xcode Target and Simulator for WatchKit*

The "Total" text is a bit long and might need to be tweaked, but the UI compiles and displays. With only a few changes, we can have a watch UI based on the iOS UI thanks to SwiftUI.

Chapter Summary

This Tip Calculator project allowed us to use some of the things we learned in a small but realistic app. By using the @State property wrapper, we used the UI to update our properties. We used other properties as data and functionality.

With a TextField and Picker, we allowed the user to enter their values. The Text items displayed the title and output tip and total.

There's a handful of padding, spacers, and other modifiers to tweak the UI just a bit.

Using this same SwiftUI code, we created a WatchKit UI. Only two small changes were required to make it compile. From there, we might want to update the UI a bit to fit better. But hopefully it was fun to see that the same code built a UI for another device.

CHAPTER 19

User Input Form

We've covered a variety of items for user input already. Some of those will be included in this chapter. They might be used in a different way or with other options, parameters, and so on.

In this chapter, we're going to build a user input form. We're going to focus on the aspects required for various pieces of input. Based on that, we'll create the user interface.

The input is based on some common types of data used in apps.

- Email String
- Monetary number (displayed as a String/currency)
- Date (displayed as a String/date)
- Selection from a list

One key factor here is that these values aren't just regular Strings and numbers. They need to be validated, formatted, listed, and otherwise processed.

Our user interface will be a form for people to input information like Figure 19-1.

© Bear Cahill 2021
B. Cahill, *UI Design for iOS App Development*,
https://doi.org/10.1007/978-1-4842-6449-2_19

Figure 19-1. *Form User Interface*

Form

A Form is a container for UI items. It is defined as a struct that conforms to the View protocol. Just like HStack, VStack, Section, or Group, a Form wraps other UI elements inside as a grouping.

A Form doesn't take any parameters or otherwise have options other than typical SwiftUI modifiers.

The unique thing about Form is how it is displayed on various platforms. As the Apple documentation describes, a Form is a "container for grouping controls used for data entry."

That's exactly what we're doing in our project. If things go well, we could use the same code in an app for other platforms.

Section

Our form will be broken up into sections. The Section item is good for this. On the iOS UI, a Form looks like a List. And a Section looks like a section in a table view.

If you look at Figure 19-1, you'll see five sections. The section for the state selection has two items that appear together in one section.

A section can be created with a header and/or footer. Otherwise, it's much like a Group or Form: returns a View to display.

Inside our various sections, we'll create a UI via elements or other groups of UI items in HStack and such.

App Requirements

Let's go over a few of the requirements of our app. We're entering an email address, monetary number, and date and making a selection from a list. We want to validate the email address, format the number into currency, and format the date.

We could use a date picker for the date, but we're going to use a String for input but store it as a Date.

For the email, we can write a validation function in an extension on String. For the currency and date fields, we'll use a number formatter and date formatter, respectively. We can create those as computed properties in an extension on each class.

For the selection from the list, we'll store the selected index in an array. So we need a list of values to choose from.

I've provided a starter project for this exercise titled InputForm. It's in a zip file titled Ch19_BOC_InputForm.zip. It contains the extensions we'll use for the formatters and for validating a String as an email (see Figure 19-2).

```
extension DateFormatter {
    static var shortDateFormatter : DateFormatter {
        let df = DateFormatter()
        df.dateStyle = .short
        df.timeStyle = .none
        return df
    }
}

extension NumberFormatter {
    static var currencyFormatter : NumberFormatter {
        let nf = NumberFormatter()
        nf.numberStyle = .currency
        nf.isLenient = true
        return nf
    }
}

extension String {
    var isValidEmail:  Bool {
        let regEx = "[A-Z0-9a-z._%+-]+@[A-Za-z0-9.-]+"
            + "\\.[A-Za-z]{2,64}"
        let pred = NSPredicate(format:
            "SELF MATCHES %@", regEx)
        let result = pred.evaluate(with: self)
        return result
    }
}
```

Figure 19-2. *Extensions Provided in the BOC Project*

FORM-BASED USER INTERFACE

Open the InputForm project provided in Ch19_BOC_InputForm.zip. Starting from there, we'll create our user input form.

1. In the ContentView struct, define properties for the list of States to choose from and where to store the email, selected state, user income, and date of birth.

Note   Only a partial list of states is provided here.

```
let states = ["Alabama", "Alaska",

    "American Samoa", "Arizona", "Arkansas",
    "California", "Colorado", "Connecticut",
    "Delaware", "District of Columbia"]

@State var email = ""
@State var selectedState = 0
@State var userIncome = 0.0
@State var dateOfBirth = Date.distantPast
```

2. Replace the current body contents with a Form.

```
var body: some View {
        Form {
            }
}
```

The first Section we'll add is for entering an email address. The TextField for this value will be pretty basic. The property is already defined; we just need the TextField.

3. Create a Section inside the Form including a TextField with binding to $email.

```
Section {
    TextField("Email", text: $email)
    { (beingEdited) in
        print (beingEdited)
    } onCommit: {
    }
}
```

The first closure, onEditingChanged, is called when the contents start and end editing. The parameter is a boolean for when the textfield contents are being edited.

When the user begins typing in the field, true will be printed. It will print false when they tap return.

The second closure is when the content is committed (i.e., the return key is tapped by the user).

So far, the UI in the Canvas preview should look like Figure 19-3.

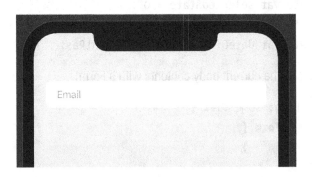

Figure 19-3. *UI with an Email TextField*

In the onCommit closure, we can validate the email address.

4. Add a check to validate the email entered in the onCommit closure.

```
Section {
    TextField("Email", text: $email)
    { (changed) in
    } onCommit: {
        if email.isValidEmail == false {
            $email.wrappedValue = ""
        }
    }
}
```

This just clears the textfield if the user enters an invalid email address.

5. Set the keyboard and content type to be .emailAddress.

```
Section {
    TextField("Email", text: $email)
    { (changed) in
    } onCommit: {
        if email.isValidEmail == false {
            $email.wrappedValue = ""
        }
    }
    .keyboardType(.emailAddress)
    .textContentType(.emailAddress)
}
```

6. Create another Section for the income input with the currency formatter provided in the NumberFormatter extension.

```
Section {
    HStack {
        TextField("Income", value: $userIncome,
        formatter: NumberFormatter.currencyFormatter)
    }
}
```

The formatter will keep the number entered as currency.

7. Add a .disabled modifier to the TextField so that it's only enabled if the user has an email address entered.

```
TextField("Income", value: $userIncome,
formatter: NumberFormatter.currencyFormatter)
.disabled(self.email.count == 0)
```

8. Add another Section with a textfield using binding to dateOfBirth and formatter of the shortDateFormatter created in the DateFormatter extension.

```
Section {
    TextField("DOB", value: $dateOfBirth,
        formatter: DateFormatter.shortDateFormatter)
}
```

The formatter, in this case, will take the dateOfBirth property (Date) and convert it to a String using the short date format and no time style. When the user enters a new value, the formatter will be used to convert that String to a date to store back in the dateOfBirth property.

9. Add another Section with a horizontal scroll view with an HStack in it. Inside the HStack, create Text items for each state in the list.

```
Section {
    ScrollView(.horizontal) {
        HStack(spacing: 40) {
            ForEach(states.indices) { index in
                Text(self.states[index])
            }
        }
    }
}
```

The HStack has a spacing value of 40 to keep the Text items nicely spaced apart.

10. Add a tap gesture to the Text item in the ForEach to set the selectedState property.

```
Text(self.states[index])
    .onTapGesture {
        self.selectedState = index
    }
```

Now as the user taps on state names, it updates the property to the corresponding array index.

11.   Change the text color for the selectedState item.

```
Text(self.states[index])
    .onTapGesture {
        self.selectedState = index
    }.foregroundColor(self.selectedState
                == index ? .black : .gray)
```

The UI with a selected state should look like Figure 19-4.

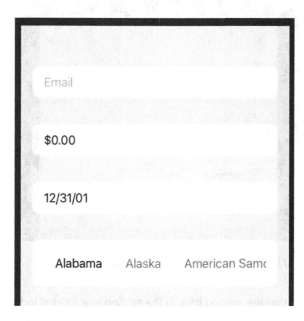

Figure 19-4. *UI with a Selected State*

Another option for selecting the state is a Picker. We'll define a picker but also add a NavigationView to drill down into it.

12. Create a Picker in the same section as the ScrollView.

```
Picker(selection: $selectedState,
       label: Text("State")) {
    ForEach(self.states.indices, id: \.self) {
        Text(self.states[$0])
    }
}
```

Now the interface looks like Figure 19-5.

Figure 19-5. *UI with Two State Items in the Section*

Notice that the second item in the section has a detail indicator (>). However, if you tap on this, nothing happens. That's because we haven't provided a way for the app to navigate.

Let's add a NavigationView to allow the app to drill down into the state selection. To do that, we need to embed our Form in a NavigationView.

13. Add a NavigationView above the Form.

```
var body: some View {
    NavigationView {
        Form {
```

14. Add a closing curly brace after the Form and a navigation title for our input form.

```
}.navigationTitle("Account Details")
```

The row for the State leads to a List (table view) when tapped as in Figure 19-6.

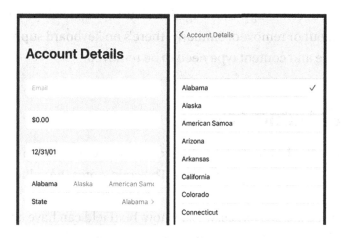

Figure 19-6. *Second State Selection Option*

We now have a form that allows the user to input values. We have multiple text-based values. However, each behaves differently based on their formatters and/or validation.

WatchKit

Another cool thing, as we saw before, is that this UI works on the Watch as well. It requires just a few changes but looks like Figure 19-7.

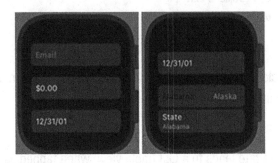

Figure 19-7. *UI on Watch*

WatchKit doesn't support NavigationView so that needs to be commented out or removed. Similarly, there's no keyboard support so the keyboard type and content type need to be removed.

Chapter Summary

In this app, we had a bit of a UI design to aim for. We needed to create an app that allowed users to enter values. The code stores the values with bindings.

Beyond storing the values, we saw how TextField can have an associated formatter like date or number formatter.

We also used a Form to display our mechanism for user input. We used Sections in our Form that are displayed in a table view.

A horizontal scroll view made one option for selecting a state pretty easy. We used an HStack with Text items. The onTapGesture for those set the selection.

A Picker combined with a NavigationView allowed us to drill down into a list for State selection.

We could probably break apart a lot of these pieces into their own structs that conform to a View. That's an exercise left up to the reader.

CHAPTER 20

Presenting Popups

It's easy to understand that we need ways for users to enter data. We have textfields, pickers, buttons, and many more ways for users to see and select items.

We also need ways to alert the user of information. If they enter an invalid email, we want to tell them. We may need to display some information or help to the user. So there are some ways of presenting messages to the user that we'll use.

Alerts, Action Sheets, Sheets, and Popovers are great ways to present the UI to the users without it being part of the base interface of the app. Each has their own aspects and user interaction.

Alert Modifier

The .alert modifier takes a binding and a closure. The binding parameter can be for a boolean (argument label isPresented as in the following code) or an optional item (argument label item) that implements Identifiable.

If called with a boolean, the alert modifier's closure is called if the value changes to true. If instead of a boolean binding it uses a binding to an optional, the closure is called when the optional is set to a non-nil value.

In either case, the closure returns an Alert instance.

```
.alert(isPresented: $showAlert) { () -> Alert in
    Alert(title: Text("Alert!"))
}
```

© Bear Cahill 2021
B. Cahill, *UI Design for iOS App Development*,
https://doi.org/10.1007/978-1-4842-6449-2_20

ALERT MODIFIER

We're going to create a new project and add various types of alerts and pop-ups to it.

1. Create a new iOS App template project named Pop-ups with SwiftUI for the interface and SwiftUI App for the life cycle.

   We want to create alerts based on various conditions. First, we'll create one based on a boolean value.

2. Add a boolean property called alert to the ContentView struct.

   ```
   @State var alert = false
   ```

3. Replace the current implementation of the body computed property with a Button. The action of the button will change the value of the alert property.

   ```
   Button("Alert!") {

       $alert.wrappedValue = true

   }
   ```

4. Add an .alert modifier to the end of the button with the isPresented bound to the $alert.

   ```
   Button("Alert!") {

       $alert.wrappedValue = true

   }

   .alert(isPresented: $alert, content: {

   })
   ```

   For the content, we want to return an Alert instance. Alert has a variety of initializers as you can see in Figure 20-1.

```
Alert(|
    M  (title:)
    M  (title:message:dismissButton:)
    M  (title:message:primaryButton:secondaryButton:)
    M  (title:primaryButton:secondaryButton:)
       (title: Text) -> Alert
       Creates an alert with one button.
```

Figure 20-1. *Alert Initializers' Code Complete*

If you just need to present some text with a default button, you only need to provide a title which is of type Text. If you also want to present a message, it's a Text also.

For any buttons you want to present, you can use the built-in Alert. Button types of default, destructive, and cancel. Each takes a Text and an optional action closure.

5. Return an Alert from the content closure.

```
.alert(isPresented: $alert, content: {
    Alert(title: Text("Alert!"),
          message: Text("You tapped the button."),
          primaryButton: .default(Text("OK")),
          secondaryButton: .cancel({
            print (alert)

        })

    )

})
```

When the button is tapped, the Alert looks like Figure 20-2.

Figure 20-2. *Alert with Two Buttons*

Notice that the secondary button is cancel. When it's tapped, it will print the alert value. It will always print false. The alert appears because we set the value to true. When one of the buttons is tapped, it will disappear and set the alert to false.

A destructive button uses red text to notify danger. If your alert is confirming a deletion or something similar, the destructive type button should be used.

Alerts are meant to give the user some information and possibly prompt them to make a decision or respond to a question. The decision should be based around the user providing input or just alerting them to some information.

Besides binding the .alert modifier to a boolean, it can be bound to an optional. When the optional is set to non-nil, the alert will display.

ALERT WITH OBJECT BINDING

Mostly this is similar to the .alert modifier with isPresented. However, we'll use an optional. When it's set to non-nil, the Alert will be presented. As with the boolean, when the user taps a button to dismiss the Alert, the value will be set back to nil.

1. Open the same project from the previous exercise.

2.   Embed the Button in the body property in a VStack.

3.   Below the Button's .alert modifier, add a Text item.

```
Text("Second")
```

We'll add the .alert modifier to this Text item. Instead of the isPresented, we'll use the initializer that takes an item. The item needs to conform to the Identifiable protocol. Let's make a struct that does that.

4.   Above the ContentView struct, create a new struct called User that implements Identifiable.

```
struct User : Identifiable {
    var id = UUID()
    var name = "Test"

}
```

Now that we have a type, we can use it as an Optional property in our ContentView.

5.   Add an Optional User type property to the ContentView struct.

```
@State var user : User?
```

6.   Set the user to an instance of User in the previous Alert's cancel button.

```
Alert(title: Text("Alert!"),

  message: Text("You tapped the button."),
  primaryButton: .default(Text("OK")),
  secondaryButton: .cancel({
    self.user = User()

  })
```

The pieces in the last three steps lay the groundwork for our alert. We'll add a .alert modifier to the Text item using the user property as the binding. When it's set to non-nil in the cancel closure, the alert will trigger.

7.   Add the .alert modifier to the Text item.

```
Text("Second")
```

```
.alert(item: $user) { (theUser) -> Alert in
    Alert(title: Text("Cancel?"),
            message: Text("\(theUser.name)")

    )

}
```

The body property code now looks like Figure 20-3.

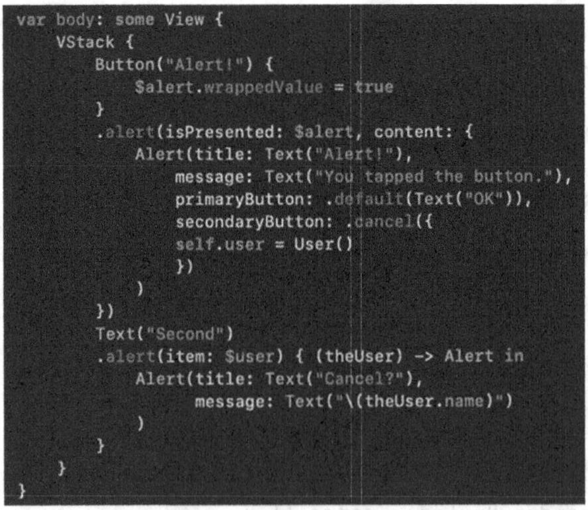

Figure 20-3. *Code with Two Alerts*

We have an .alert modifier bound to the user. When it's set to non-nil, the closure will get called to create the Alert. The user is passed in as the parameter: theUser.

The title is "Cancel?" and we set the message to the user's name. The Alert will use an automatically provided "OK" button to dismiss.

Since the User struct has a default value of Test for the name property, the alert looks like Figure 20-4.

Figure 20-4. *Alert with Default OK Button*

Now we've seen both binding types for the .alert modifier and a couple variations of Alert.

Action Sheet Modifier

The .actionSheet modifier is very similar to the .alert modifier. It can use a binding for a bool (isPresented) or optional (item). The second parameter is a closure, but it returns an ActionSheet instead of an Alert.

The closure will be called if the binding value goes true (for Boolean binding) or non-nil (for optional binding).

Action Sheet

Creating an ActionSheet is similar to an Alert. You can pass in a Text item as the title parameter. If you only provide a title parameter value, the action sheet automatically includes a Cancel button to remove the action sheet.

The message parameter is also a Text and is optional. The last parameter is an array of buttons. There are variations of the button you can use as in Figure 20-5.

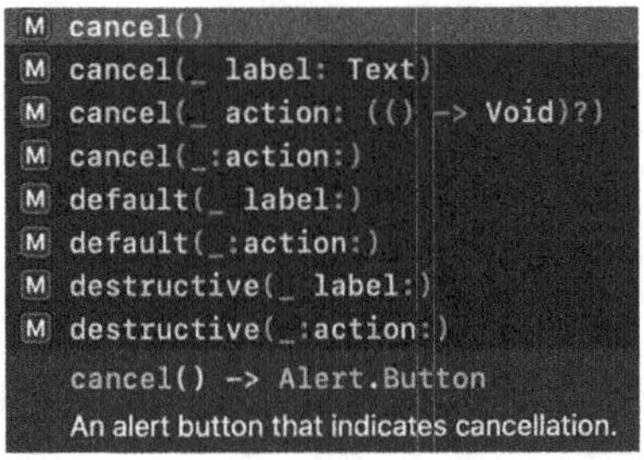

Figure 20-5. *Variations of Action Sheet Buttons*

The cancel button without parameters simply removes the action sheet from the UI. The action parameter allows you to pass in a closure to be called when the button is tapped. All other variations of the buttons require a Text item to display on the button and an optional closure to call when the button is tapped.

ACTION SHEET MODIFIER

This exercise is built on top of the previous exercise and uses the same project. However, a new project would also work since this exercise doesn't rely on anything previously done.

1. Add a new boolean property to the ContentView.

   ```
   @State var actionSheet = false
   ```

2. In the VStack (or the body if a new project), add a Button. The action of the button sets the property from step 1 to true.

```
Button("Action Sheet") {

    $actionSheet.wrappedValue = true

}
```

3. Add an .actionSheet modifier at the end of the Button.

```
.actionSheet(isPresented: $actionSheet, content: {

})
```

4. Return an ActionSheet from the content closure of the .actionSheet.

```
.actionSheet(isPresented: $actionSheet, content: {

    ActionSheet(title: Text("Action"),

                message: Text("Go!"),
                buttons:
                    [.destructive(Text("Delete"))]

    )

})
```

Running the code presents a button titled "Action Sheet." When it's tapped, the actionSheet property is set to true.

The .actionSheet modifier is bound to that property and will be triggered.

The ActionSheet created is then displayed with the buttons, in this case one destructive button, on the screen as in Figure 20-6.

299

Figure 20-6. *ActionSheet with One Button*

There is a small but meaningful difference between an alert and an action sheet. An alert is limited to one or two buttons and usually focused on providing information. An action sheet should result in

some "action" taking place: saving data, sending information online, deleting a user account, and other functionality based on the user's selection.

Sheet Modifier

Sheet is similar to what we've already seen with Alert and ActionSheet. It takes a binding to a boolean (isPresented) or optional (item). It also has an optional closure called onDismiss. This closure, if passed in, will be called when the action sheet is removed from the UI.

The final parameter is a closure to define the UI on the sheet. This closure, like the body parameter, returns an item implementing a View. So it's not a specific UI element like Alert or ActionSheet. It's anything that implements a View.

SHEET MODIFIER

Again, this is building on the previous project but isn't necessary.

1. Add a boolean property to ContentView to bind to the sheet.

```
@State var sheet = false
```

2. Add a button that sets the property to true.

```
Button("Sheet") {

    $sheet.wrappedValue = true

}
```

3. Add a .sheet modifier bound to the property and that returns a VStack.

```
.sheet(isPresented: $sheet, content: {

    VStack {

    }

})
```

4. In the VStack, add a Text and Button to set the property back to false.

```
.sheet(isPresented: $sheet, content: {
    VStack {
        Text ("Tap to Dismiss")
        Button("Dismiss") {
            $sheet.wrappedValue = false

        }

    }

})
```

Setting the property back to false will cause the sheet to dismiss. The UI will adapt to the device/screen space it's running on. On the iPhone, it will look like Figure 20-7. In this case, dragging down will also dismiss the sheet's UI.

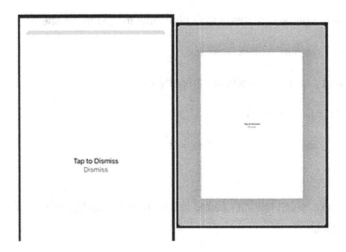

Figure 20-7. *Sheet UI Displayed on iPhone and iPad*

Sheet is a good option for displaying the UI more modal/fullscreen compared to Alert and ActionSheet. It can certainly be much more custom since it just needs to implement a View.

Popover Modifier

Popover is created similar to what we've already seen with alert, action sheet, and sheet. Like a Sheet, it takes a binding either boolean (isPresented) or optional (item). It also takes a closure to return the UI to display.

Optionally, .popover takes an anchor point and arrow edge parameters. The anchor point defines where the popover is attached. It can be a point or a rect. The arrow edge specifies where the arrow of the popover is displayed.

For smaller UI devices (e.g., iPhone), the popover will be displayed modally and look like the Sheet in Figure 20-7. This is the case regardless of values for the anchor and arrow.

In some cases, the layout will prevent the UI from respecting the anchor and arrow settings. In that case, or if they aren't provided, the system will decide how to display the popover.

POPOVER MODIFIER

Again, using the same project, we'll create a new property, button, and popover modifier.

1. Add a new boolean property to ContentView for binding to the .popover modifier.

```
@State var popover = false
```

2. Add a Button in the body VStack to set the property to true.

```
Button("Popover") {

    $popover.wrappedValue = true

}
```

3. Add a .popover modifier to the Button bound to the new property with settings for the attachment anchor, arrow edge, and content that returns a View conforming to the UI item.

```
.popover(isPresented: $popover,
        attachmentAnchor: .point(.trailing),
        arrowEdge: .leading,
        content: {

    Text("Popover! Here we are just...")
```

```
        .lineLimit(2)

        .frame(width: 300, height: 300,
        alignment: .center)

    })
```

On iPhone and small devices/screens, it looks like a Sheet, but on iPad/larger screens, it pops up with a context arrow as in Figure 20-8.

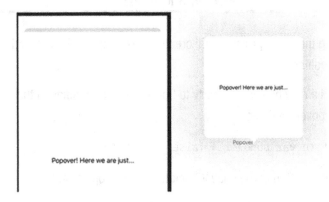

Figure 20-8. *Popover Displayed on iPhone and iPad*

Popovers are great for displaying information contextually. If you have a message for the user based on something in the UI, popover gives you a great option especially for the iPad.

Chapter Summary

Alerts, Action Sheets, Sheets, and Popovers are all bound to a value and presented based on that value whether it's a boolean or Identifiable.

There's a variety of options for how these items are displayed in your app.

The .alert modifier returns an Alert. It can have one or two buttons with or without closures.

The .actionSheet modifier returns an ActionSheet which can have many buttons. If there are too many for the screen size, it will scroll.

For the .sheet modifier, we have an onDismiss closure. The UI for the .sheet isn't a specific type. It's just something that implements a View so it can be an HStack, VStack, Text, or various other elements.

Similar to .sheet, .popover has a closure that returns something that conforms to View. In cases where the UI is smaller (e.g., iPhone or iPad with only partial screen display), .popover and .sheet will appear the same. But on larger UI instances, popover will be displayed near the tapped UI like a callout. It may be to the side or top/bottom and have an arrow to the initiating element.

APPENDIX A

Cheat Sheets

I find myself often looking back at content I've read for key pieces of information. Typically it's a code example that I can remember vaguely but need to see the details: a method call, modifier name or parameters.

This appendix is a collection of cheats based on each chapter to show you how some examples worked without having to hunt for them. Also, it can serve as notes of the code examples and, in that, of the book.

Chapter 2: Take It Easy

Modifiers - Modifiers area used on various UI elements to modify the appearance. They can be added in code or with the **SwiftUI Attributes Inspector** ($^\wedge \smallsmile$ + click).

```
Text("Hello, SwiftUI!")
    .font(.largeTitle)
    .fontWeight(.bold)
    .foregroundColor(Color.purple)
    .padding(30.0)
    .frame(width: 200.0, height: 400.0)
    .background(Color.orange)
    .cornerRadius(40.0)
```

Stacks - HStack and VStack are common ways to group UI elements horizontally and vertically respectively.

© Bear Cahill 2021
B. Cahill, *UI Design for iOS App Development*,
https://doi.org/10.1007/978-1-4842-6449-2

Chapter 3: SwiftUI Building Blocks

Button - Buttons are typically created with two parameters: what do show and what to do. One way is with the action (closure) first and label (View) is second. Another is with a String first and action second.

```
Button(action: {
    print ("tapped!")
}, label: { Text("Tap Me") })
```

Image - This creates an image to display in the UI created with a name, system name or other initializers.

```
Image(systemName: "camera")
```

Toggle - A binary (on/off) UI input item (e.g., UISwift).

@State wrapper - This creates a wrapper for binding a local variable as a source of truth.

```
Toggle(isOn: $isReady,
      label: {
      Text("Ready: " + (isReady ? "Yes" : "No"))

})
```

TextField - Input UI element for user to enter text.

```
TextField("Username", text:$username)
```

Chapter 4: Binding Source of Truth

Strideable - This protocol extends Comparable (which extends Equatable) and provides the interface for distance and advancedBy.

@Binding wrapper - Speicifies that a value passed into an object is the source of truth.

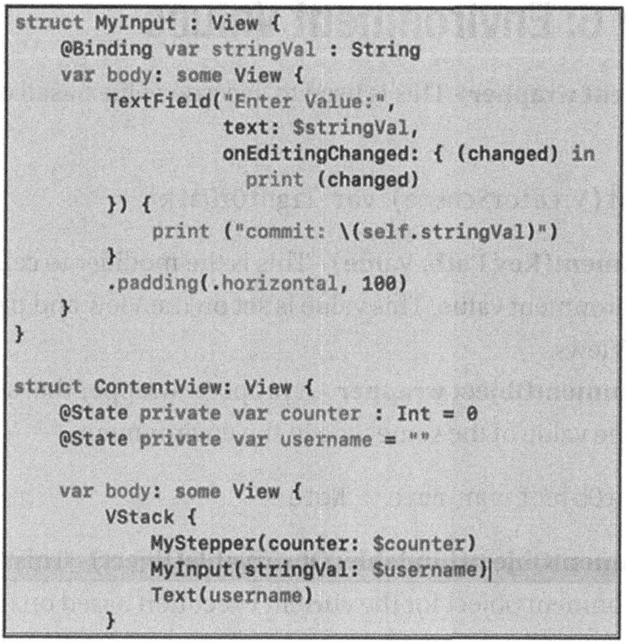

```
struct MyInput : View {
    @Binding var stringVal : String
    var body: some View {
        TextField("Enter Value:",
                  text: $stringVal,
                  onEditingChanged: { (changed) in
                      print (changed)
        }) {
            print ("commit: \(self.stringVal)")
        }
        .padding(.horizontal, 100)
    }
}

struct ContentView: View {
    @State private var counter : Int = 0
    @State private var username = ""

    var body: some View {
        VStack {
            MyStepper(counter: $counter)
            MyInput(stringVal: $username)|
            Text(username)
        }
```

Figure A-1. *MyInput Struct and Updated ContentView body*

Chapter 5: ObservableObjects

ObservableObject - This is a protocol for objects that external objects will bind as a source of truth.

  @ObservedObject wrapper - This is a wrapper for an object implementing ObserverableObject to be bound as a fourth of truth.

  @Published wrapper - This wrapper specifies a property in an ObservableObject to be published when changed.

  objectWillChange.send() - This call can be used in place of @Publised to publish changes from an ObservableObject.

Chapter 6: Environment Values

@Environment wrapper - This is used to access a value based on a key path.

```
@Environment(\.colorScheme) var lightOrDark
```

   .environment(Key Path, Value) - This is the modifier to call on a View to set an environment value. This value is set on the View and passed down to any child Views.

   @EnvironmentObject wrapper - A property wrapper that sets the property to the value of the same type in the environment.

```
@EnvironmentObject var note : Note
```

   .environmentObject(bindable: ObservableObject) - This modifier sets an environment object for the current execution based on its type.

Chapter 7: List of Items

List - UI grouping that displays the View items created in the closure in a list of rows.

```
List {
    ForEach(notes) { note in
        NoteRow(note: note, df: self.df)
    }
    .onDelete { offsets in
        self.notes.remove(atOffsets: offsets)
    }
}
```

Chapter 8: SwiftUI Canvas Preview

PreviewProvider - This is the protocol the preview needs to implement which requires a "previews" property.

.previewDevice(Preview Device String) - This modifier takes a device String value to display that device's preview.

```
Group {
    ForEach(ContentSizeCategory.allCases,
        id: \.self) { sizeCat in
            ContentView()
                .environment(\.colorScheme, .dark)
                .environment(\.sizeCategory, sizeCat)
    }
    ContentView()
        .previewDevice("iPhone 8")
    ContentView()
        .previewDevice("iPhone 11")
}
```

Chapter 9: Design for Previews

Preview Content group - This project group contains files and assets to be used in the previews.

Live Mode - This mode effectively runs the app in the Canvas.

Chapter 10: SwiftUI Navigation

.onTapGesture - This modifier takes a closure to call when the UI element is tapped.

.sheet - This modifier is presented based on a binding for the first parameter (item (Optional) or isPresented (Bool)). The second parameter is a closure returning a View to display.

```
.sheet(item: $selectedNoteVM) { (noteVM) in
    Text(noteVM.text)
}
```

NavigationView - This element returns a View that may have elements including a NavigationLink.

NavigationLink - This UI item has a variety of initializers to specify something to tap and something to display via navigation when tapped.

```
NavigationView {
    NavigationLink("Tap Here", destination:
        Text("Display Me Next")
        .navigationTitle("Title"))
}
```

Chapter 11: UIKit in SwiftUI

UIViewRepresentable - This protocol inherits from View and declares makeUIView, updateUIView and dismantleUIView functions. It's implementation of View includes a Body type of Never so it doesn't return a View.

makeUIView - This protocol function takes a Context and returns a UIView.

updateUIView - This protocol function takes a Context and whatever makeUIView returns. It is meant to update the view passed in.

dismantleUIView - This protocol function takes the UIView created by makeUIView and a Coordinator. It is meant to clean up the elements before removal from the UI.

Chapter 12: Data from UIKit with Coordinator

Coordinator - This custom type is passed around in the Context for the UIViewRepresentable object. It facilitates the UIKit relationships (e.g., delegate) for SwiftUI.

makeCoordinator - This protocol function returns an instance of the customer Coordinator.

```
struct TextView: UIViewRepresentable {
    @Binding var text: String

    func makeUIView(context: Context) -> UITextView {
        let tv = UITextView()
        tv.delegate = context.coordinator
        return tv
    }

    func updateUIView(_ tvNote: UITextView, context: Context) {
        tvNote.text = text
    }

    func makeCoordinator() -> TextView.Coordinator {
        Coordinator(text: $text)
    }

    class Coordinator: NSObject, UITextViewDelegate {
        var text: Binding<String>

        init(text: Binding<String>) {
            self.text = text
        }

        func textViewDidChange(_ textView: UITextView) {
            text.wrappedValue = textView.text
        }
    }
}
```

Figure A-2. *TextView with Coordinator Class*

Chapter 14: SwiftUI in UIKit

UIHostingController - This UIKit view controller subclass is created with an NSCoder and SwiftUI View to display via Storyboard navigation.

313

showDetails - This Interface Builder segue action function takes an NSCoder and expects a UIViewController (Optional) returned. A UIHostingController make be created and returned.

```
@IBSegueAction func showDetails(_ coder: NSCoder)
      -> UIViewController? {
   return UIHostingController(coder: coder,
      rootView: swiftUIView)
}
```

Chapter 15: Introduction to Combine

Publisher - Defines output and failure type and has subscribers.

Subscriber - Defines input and failure type and has receive methods.

Sink Subscriber - Takes two closures: completion and receive value.

Assign Subscriber - Takes a key path and an instance to assign the value in using that key path.

Chapter 16: URLSession Publisher

URLSession - dataTaskPublisher function returns a Publisher for a URL or URLRequest.

decode - Function that takes a type and Coder (e.g., JSONDecoder) to handle the URL response.

Chapter 17: Transitions and Animation

transition - Modifier to change the position of a UI element

animation - Modifier to add animation to visual changes.

asymmetric - Transition modifier to insert and remove UI elements in two different styles.

withAnimation - Function to specify changes to occur with animation.

rotationEffect - 2D rotation change to a UI element.

rotation3DEffect - 3D rotation around specified 3D axis.

DrawingGroup - Renders a composite of UI changes offscreen first for performance.

Chapter 20: Presenting Pop-Ups

alert - Modifier taking a boolean or Optional to determine if the alert presents if it's true or non-nil respectively. Returns an Alert instance.

Alert - Struct taking a Text item to display when applicable.

Action Sheet - Modifier to display a View with various action variations.

Sheet - Modifier taking a boolean or Optional to determine if the sheet is presented if it's true or non-nil respectively. Takes a closure that returns a View to display.

Popover - Modifier taking a boolean or Optional to determine if the sheet is presented if it's true or non-nil respectively. It can also take input for displaying an arrow to the UI causing the popover on larger devices.

Index

A

ActionSheet, 297, 298
  modifier, 298–300
  variations, 298
.addTarget function, 182, 189
.alert modifier, 291–294, 296, 297
allCases, 131, 221
Animations, 252, 253
App requirements, 194, 279, 280
Asymmetric transition, 249, 250

B

@Binding
  ContentView, 56
  counter property, 56, 57
  MyStepper
    implementation, 56
    initializer, 56, 57
    instances, 57
    struct, 55, 56
  Textfield, 58
    binding property, 58
    body property, 59
    MyInput struct, 59, 60
    MyStepper, 59
    MyTextInput, 58

    onCommit, 59
    onEditingChanged, 59
    String property, 59
    Text item, 59
    UI, 60, 61
  UI elements, 55
  View types, 56
Building blocks, SwiftUI
  binding, 34
  button
    auto-complete code, 28, 29
    computed property, 28
    creation, 28
    label, 29
    output, 30
    parameters, 31
    Text item, 29
  image, 31
    creation, 32, 33
    SF symbols, 31
  standard elements, 27
  @State property
    wrapper, 34, 35
  TextField
    add, 43–47
    compile/run, 41
    Object Library, 40–42

© Bear Cahill 2021
B. Cahill, *UI Design for iOS App Development*,
https://doi.org/10.1007/978-1-4842-6449-2

Printed in the United States
By Bookmasters